Taiji as Moving Meditation

of related interest

Tàijíquán
Li Deyin
ISBN 978 0 85701 403 0

The Five Levels of Taijiquan
Grandmaster Chen Xiaowang
Commentary by Master Jan Silberstorff
ISBN 978 1 84819 093 1
eISBN 978 0 85701 079 7

The Essence of Taijiquan Push-Hands and Fighting Technique
Wang Fengming
ISBN 978 1 84819 245 4
eISBN 978 0 85701 190 9

Tai Ji Dancing for Kids
Five Moving Forces
Chungliang Al Huang with Lark Huang-Storms and Sylvia Yulan Storms
ISBN 978 1 84819 372 7
eISBN 978 0 85701 329 3

Climbing the Steps to Qincheng Mountain
A Practical Guide to the Path of Daoist Meditation and Qigong
Wang Yun
ISBN 978 1 78775 076 0
eISBN 978 1 78775 077 7

Taiji as Moving Meditation

Fundamental Principles and Practices

Paul G. Fendos, Jr.

SINGING DRAGON
LONDON AND PHILADELPHIA

First published in 2019
by Singing Dragon
an imprint of Jessica Kingsley Publishers
73 Collier Street
London N1 9BE, UK
and
400 Market Street, Suite 400
Philadelphia, PA 19106, USA

www.singingdragon.com

Library of Congress Cataloging in Publication Data
A CIP catalog record for this book is available from the Library of Congress

British Library Cataloguing in Publication Data
A CIP catalogue record for this book is available from the British Library

ISBN 978 1 78775 043 2
eISBN 978 1 78775 044 9

Printed and bound in the United States

The accompanying videos can be downloaded from
www.jkp.com/voucher using the code BUEZURE

To

Jin Jong-baek 陳鍾白

Teacher and Master

33rd Generation Disciple of the Shaolin Temple

Contents

Preface

I have spent the greater part of the last 40-plus years studying East Asia. An important part of that effort has focused on the martial arts, which have become an integral part of my daily life. As I have aged, I have come to appreciate the practice of Taiji, a Chinese soft martial art that offers its practitioners the opportunity to maintain skills and conditioning while also developing what might best be called a greater spiritual awareness—increased perception of one's surroundings, as well as an inner quiet that opens the door to a new appreciation of life and a greater sense of wellbeing. With China and things Chinese becoming the object of more and closer examination by an increasingly wide range of readers—including a growing number of people looking for time-tested East Asian forms of exercise and healing—now seems the opportune time to offer this new look at Taiji and its place in the culture of exercise and health.

Taiji really is a unique form of exercise, one not difficult to learn, and one that functions to replace stress with relaxation, anxiety with calm and peace of mind. Described by some as an adjunct to regular medical care that contributes to the prevention and rehabilitation of many conditions associated with both injury and age, Taiji has been shown to enhance aerobic capacity and muscle strength, giving one greater energy and stamina, while improving flexibility, agility, coordination, and balance. It also helps lower blood pressure naturally, promoting greater heart health, and reduces chronic inflammation, ameliorating such conditions as arthritis. It is even said to ease levels of depression. No doubt as a result of all of these things, Taiji and its system of mundane practices and concrete goals is fast overtaking general aerobics, strength training, and stretching and flexibility exercises like Yoga as the activity of choice for many people, including the elderly, for whom it may very well be the future of fitness. One cannot go wrong by studying this art and I wholeheartedly recommend it to all.

In ending, a few words of special thanks. To those who contributed most to my understanding and knowledge of martial arts—Anthony DeSardi, Lee Baek-Oon, An Hak-son, and Chin Jong-baek. And for their help in facilitating the publication of this book—James Cherry (Commissioning Editor), Victoria Peters (Production Manager), and Madeleine Budd (Editorial Assistant), all of Jessica Kingsley Publishers.

Paul G. Fendos, Jr.
September 2018

Accessing Videos

A total of ten videos accompany this book, each given a name that reflects its content. These ten videos, from which all still shots are taken and references to which can be found in the different sections of the book, cover everything from an easy-to-learn warm-up to basic moves and the Forms that they make up. A **Taiji as Moving Meditation "Read Me First"** document is also provided to help practitioners of Taiji better understand and utilize these videos.

The videos can be accessed by going to www.jkp.com/voucher. On that webpage create an account using your email address and a password. Then log in to your account and redeem the following voucher code, which will allow you to download the videos: BUEZURE.

1

Introduction

Along with the Chinese character, Confucius, and the Great Wall, the slow rhythmical form of exercise we know as Taiji[1] has become almost synonymous with China. However, in the United States and numerous other countries little is really widely known about it. In fact, most people are unaware that worldwide upwards of 250 million men and women of all ages have already joined the growing movement to learn Taiji, some as part of a rigorous regime for international tournaments and competitions, but most for the various health benefits it is thought to confer. Even a cursory look at its history and philosophy tells us a lot about Taiji and what it might add to our lives.

The earliest use of the word Taiji can be found in the *Book of Changes*, the central philosophical work of the Chinese tradition. As most evidence suggests that the *Book of Changes* probably originated during the 4th–3rd centuries BCE, some people have concluded that the beginnings of Taiji may also very well date to that time. However, this is just not the case. Although its origins are indeed ancient, other than the general belief that Taiji originated sometime during the second millennium of the Christian era, there is no real consensus on exactly when it began.

This general lack of consensus is due, in part, to disagreement over who might have been the first to initiate practices that can clearly be associated with Taiji. One common theory asserts that such practices most likely originated with Zhang Sanfeng, a legendary 13th-century Daoist monk. An expert in numerous fighting styles and weapons, he was a practitioner of "Internal Boxing," a system of fighting that utilized

---

1   Also referred to as *Taijiquan*, or "Fist of Taiji," in China and much of the rest of the world.

soft movements to avoid and counter strong attacks. Another theory claims it was created by Chen Wangting (1597–1644), a general and skilled martial artist who combined his military experience, knowledge of traditional Chinese medicine, and other popular teachings to establish the Chen school of Taiji. Whatever the case, its association with these two men convincingly demonstrates that in its earliest stages Taiji was essentially another form or school of martial arts.

Today numerous styles of Taiji are practiced. The Chen style, characterized by both fast and slow movements as well as short bursts of power, is still quite popular, especially among martial arts enthusiasts. However, both in East Asia and the West it is the Yang style, a Chen-style offshoot established by Yang Luchan (1799–1872), that is now most likely to be associated with Taiji. With its soft fluid movements and unwavering stances, this style might best be described as the quintessential form of modern Taiji. The Hao-Wu, the Sun, and the Wu styles, all of which can trace their origins to the Chen and Yang schools, are also widely practiced, but often, it seems, to supplement and enhance the study of the Chen or Yang styles.

In addition to these five traditional schools, there is a more recent style, aptly referred to as "New Style Taiji," that is growing in popularity. Closest in form to the Yang School, this style really combines elements of multiple schools. It is an important development in the field and a school of practice that anyone wishing to become part of the Taiji movement will no doubt want to learn. Associated with the International *Wushu* Federation, it provides the best overall systematic approach to studying Taiji in terms of fundamental practices and Forms, while offering a clear framework for helping interested practitioners advance in their study of this art. The Forms introduced in this book are part of the New Style regimen.

The philosophy of Taiji is centered on the concept embodied in its name—usually translated as the "Great Absolute." This philosophy assumes a world in which all phenomena in nature can be explained in terms of *Qi*,[2] the Vital Energy emanating from the Great Absolute, and the two Primary Modes of creation which arise from that Vital Energy—the *Yin* and the *Yang*. The *Yin* and *Yang* are contrasting yet complementary forces, perhaps best understood as representations of a Principle of Opposites on which they are based. Within the context of Taiji

---

2   Also written as *Chi* (pronounced Chee).

as exercise and meditation, all movements can be seen as reflections of this Principle of Opposites. Steps can be seen as advancing or retreating, movements of the limbs as extending or retracting, breathing as exhaling or inhaling, and striking and blocking techniques as being hard or soft. Practiced correctly—that is to say synchronized and in harmony with this Principle of Opposites—one slowly begins to cultivate the Vital Energy that is said to permeate the world, acquiring, in the process, the benefits this energy is thought to bestow—vigor, strength, and longevity, but also focus and peace of mind.

Although Taiji could very well be described as a simple form of exercise, it is not lacking in challenges, physical or intellectual. The practice of Taiji can develop into a robust daily form of exercise, working to enhance bodily control, flexibility, balance, and coordination. In addition, although the successful practice of Taiji does not require belief in any particular religious or philosophical system,[3] as Chapter 2 of this book will show, a comparison of Taiji with another system of thought or practice, classic Yoga and the breathing techniques associated with it, will help one to better understand the underlying dynamic of Taiji. This much is evident. Young or old, male or female, everyone can benefit from a program in Taiji, without fear of injury, while exercising almost every part of the body. Actually, for many, Taiji, with its subtle combination of physical movements and deep breathing, may very well be that elusive simple way to a better life they have long been searching for.

---

3   Such as Daoism, or the Great Absolute and *Yin/Yang* mentioned just above.

2

Taiji as Moving Meditation

Taiji is often referred to as "moving meditation." That is so, for the most part, because it is seen as combining concentration, breathing, and movement, activities usually found separately or together in other forms of meditation, into the fluid and rhythmical form so characteristic of this type of exercise. Taiji is likened to Yoga, of which some people consider it an offshoot—a product of the introduction of elements of Hindu or Buddhist philosophy and practice into China from India. Although clearly establishing any such link is not possible, a simple comparison of the very general theories and practices of Taiji and *classic Indian* Yoga does serve to highlight some of the similarities and differences between them as forms of meditation, something that helps make understanding and practicing Taiji easier.

Taiji[1]

Concentration

As a general rule, four main things are stressed in the practice of Taiji: the internal, the external, the upper, and the lower.

> ...the student must pay attention to the internal, the external, the upper, and the lower. That belonging to the internal refers to none other than "using the mind rather than force," below the *Qi* sinking to the lower abdomen, above the neck relaxing and the head straightening; and that belonging to the external is the lightening and invigorating of the whole body, the interconnectedness of the limbs, from the feet to the legs to the waist, and the dropping of the shoulders and bending of the elbows and the like. (Yang Chengfu 1997a, p.312)[2]

And while all four of these things are important, maybe none is emphasized more than the first, "using the mind rather than force." Unfortunately, exactly what this means is not easy to understand. Perhaps the best way to discuss it is by reference to the term "concentration." What is this concentration, though? How is it achieved? And why is it so important to the practice of Taiji?

In the context of Taiji, concentration is something more than the commonly accepted definition of it. That is to say, it is more than just "directing one's thoughts or attention to something." It is, instead, "the coalescence of the will into oneness, the congealing of the spirit... [something] preceded by a cleansing of the mind and a freeing of the mind from worry, by an elimination of reckless thought, and by the pacification of the mind and a stilling of the breath" (Chen Xin 1997a, p.260).

---

1   Assuming a history of no less than 400 years, a conservative assumption based on the supposition that its origins can be traced back at least to Chen Wangting, one would expect there to be a wealth of source materials on Taiji to choose from. Unfortunately, such is not the case. There are, though, two good collections that contain multiple introductory works dealing with the practice of Taiji. One is *The Complete Book of Taijiquan*, a Chinese-language compilation of essays, old and new, general and specific, on some of the theories and forms of the five traditional schools or styles of Taiji. The other is "Peter Lim's [English-language] online *Taijiquan* Resource Page," perhaps the single most comprehensive English-language attempt to systematically organize and introduce materials dealing with the history, theory, and practice of Taiji. Both collections are referenced in the following short explanation of Taiji.

2   All translations of Chinese materials quoted in this book are the author's (thus excluding short excerpts from Peter Lim's English-language materials).

But it also seems to be an attempt to link the conscious mind with the movements of the body.

> In practicing *Taijiquan* the focus is on the spirit, thus it is said: "The spirit is the commander, the body the servant." When the spirit can achieve this, then the movements will naturally be light and invigorated. As for the frames, they will only be empty and solid, open and closed. Opened does not mean that only the hands and feet will be opened, but the mind will also be opened with them; and closed does not mean that only the hands and feet will be closed, but the mind will also be closed with them. If the internal and the external can be harmonized as one breath, then oneness is achieved. (Yang Chengfu 1997b, p.315)[3]

And the key to establishing this link is in focusing internal consciousness on external movements.

> External form and the activity of *Qi* are a manifestation of the mind and *Qi* in the external... The integral component of this manifestation of the mind and *Qi* in the external is mainly the focusing of internal consciousness on external movements... (Editorial Committee PPEP 1997b, p.8)

Why is such concentration so important to the practice of Taiji? Because only through concentration can the *Qi*[4] be developed, and only when the *Qi* is developed is there real power or strength—along with the health-giving benefits that follow.

> When the mind arrives, then *Qi* will arrive; when *Qi* arrives, then strength will come of itself. (Yang Chengfu 1997a, p.313)

Again, though, how this is achieved—how such strength is produced—is not all that clear. General opinion suggests two possible explanations. Either concentration on the movements of Taiji helps one to open a source of power and strength (*Qi*) theretofore untapped, or the mind,

---

3   Note that further explanations of what is meant by frames, along with the empty and solid, are given below.

4   A note on *Qi*. As will be seen below, it is thought to be more than just the air we breathe. Some call it the "inner" breath, the "original" breath, or the "central" breath. What is it? No one, it seems, has clearly explained or defined it. Many believe it is related to the human nervous system, perhaps electrons. Others say it is a special secretion of the body. Some even believe that it is a combination of these two. See Editorial Committee PPEP 1997b, p.7.

through a visualization of bodily movements, gives rise to a power and strength lacking in the unguided body.[5]

One thing is clear. Most, if not all, practitioners of Taiji agree that the mind is the starting point, not force or the *Qi* from which this force arises. And if anyone attempts to compel his/her movements, to use force rather than the mind—in other words, if anyone tries to concentrate on moving the *Qi* instead of just using the mind to concentrate on external movements—then the body will become slow, stiff, and without real force or strength.

> The mind [should be] on the spirit, not on the *Qi*. If [the mind is] on the *Qi* then there will be obstruction. When practicing Taijiquan one cannot just think about the *Qi* being in the body and how to move it, but one must take one's mind and [with it] concentrate on the movements... (Editorial Committee PPEP 1997b, p.8)

> If one does not use force but uses the mind, then where the mind arrives, the *Qi* will also go there; and if like this, then the *Qi* and blood will flow freely, everyday unobstructed, throughout the whole body, never with congestion. (Yang Chengfu 1997b, p.315)

I like to think of this whole process as being one of letting go of the self, of not consciously attempting to carry out any one movement or series of movements, but just letting the body take over for you. The self, as a result, then becomes conscious only of the movements that are being practiced—in essence becomes the movements themselves.[6] How does that explain the force or strength said to result from this concentration? It does not. But it makes it easier for one to understand exactly what state of mind this concentration is supposed to bring about.

---

5   The body of evidence suggests that most Taiji masters recognize the former interpretation as the correct one. However, Chen Yanling makes the following statement: "In *Taijiquan* the use of *Yi* [mind] and *Qi* for the beginner is very difficult...for example, if we use both hands to perform a push movement, we imagine there is an opponent in front of us. Actually, at this time [standing ready?] there is no *Qi* in the palms to release. But when we start to [consciously?] imagine [what we are doing?], our *Qi* rises up the spine to the shoulders, arms, wrists, and palms, finally being released to the opponent's body" (1995a, p.1). This argues for the latter interpretation (although, as my use of brackets shows, this translation from Peter Lim's website is somewhat vague).

6   There is, of course, a certain common sense to this. The basketball player shooting a free throw does not think about shooting it, but just concentrates on shooting it. The same could be said for a batter waiting for a pitcher's pitch, an archer taking aim, and so on. All of which gives a new sense or interpretation to a very modern catch phrase: "Just do it."

Breathing

Another important element of Taiji is breathing. As concerns the four main elements stressed in the practice of Taiji (the internal, external, upper, and lower), breathing has been mentioned in the context of the internal and the lower. Breathing is, when compared with concentration, somewhat easier to understand. It is, therefore, something easier to explain. Simply stated, anyone interested in learning Taiji must know at least two things about it: how to breathe and exactly how many types of "breath" there are.

The former question, the easier of the two, might best be answered in two parts. The first part deals with the issue of orifices and through which orifice(s) breathing should occur. On this there are at least two opinions. Yang Chengfu states that "the mouth should remain half open, half closed, with inhalation through the nose, exhalation through the mouth" (1997a, p.312). While Chen Yanling asserts that the "basic breathing of *Taijiquan* should be done mostly through the nose, not the mouth…[and] thus differs from the common people who use the nose to inhale and exhale through the mouth" (1995b, p.1). The second part concerns the rhythm of breathing, and on this there is a general consensus. Breathing should be done naturally.

…inhale through the nose, exhale through the mouth, letting them follow their natural [pattern]… (Yang Chengfu 1997a, p.312)

Inhaling and exhaling [should] follow their natural [pattern]. (Chen Xin 1997b, p.287)

Otherwise, one will pant and gasp and lose one's balance when practicing.

…in one movement, in one turn of the body, whether kicking or twisting the waist, panting of breath and wavering balance, such problems all come from obstructing the breath or forcing things. (Yang Chengfu 1997a, p.312)

However, to "breathe naturally" is another one of those phrases the meaning of which is not all that clear. Chen Xin made several comments on it:

Harmonize the breathing endlessly. (1997b, p.287)

The mind and the breath are interdependent. (1997b, p.287)

One opening, one closing, all is natural. (1997a, p.260)

Standing alone, though, these comments do not contribute much to understanding what this phrase really means. In an attempt to clarify its meaning, the idea of breathing naturally is further expounded on in the section below on Movement.

The second question—how many types of breath are there?—is not so easy to answer. On the one hand, it is clear that "breath" and "breathing" often refer to respiration, the simple inhaling and exhaling of air. This certainly seems to be the case when reference is made to "breathing through the nose (or mouth)." However, the term *Qi*, generally understood as the almost mystical force said to result from concentration on external movements, is also separately used to refer to the air that we breathe.[7] Stranger still, often the term *Qi* is used to mean both things simultaneously.

Chen Yanling is a good example of someone who uses the term *Qi* in both ways (1995b, pp.1–2). He starts out by stating there are two kinds of *Qi* circulating within the body, one the upper level or post-birth *Qi*, the other the lower level or pre-birth *Qi*. When discussing respiration, Chen describes inhaling air in terms of the "upper *Qi* entering from the nose while the lower *Qi* rises in the spine from the lower abdomen to the area between the shoulder blades." And he describes exhaling air in terms of the "upper *Qi* exiting the nose while the lower *Qi* sinks into the lower abdomen." But Chen also discusses two methods of circulating the "inner *Qi*" using similar terms. First is the pre-birth to post-birth method, which moves the *Qi* "from front to back, meaning that the *Qi* from the lower abdomen travels down to the perineum and reverses to the tailbone, travels along the spine to the base of the neck, up to the crown of the head, down the forehead to the nose and raphe of the upper lip, to the throat, chest, navel and finally back to the lower abdomen." Second is the post-birth to pre-birth method, which moves the *Qi* "from back to front, meaning that the *Qi* from the lower abdomen heads up from the navel to the chest, throat, raphe of the upper lip, and forehead, reaching the crown of the head, then moving down to the base of the neck and continuing along the spine to the tailbone, until it finally reaches the perineum and returns to the lower abdomen." It is clear that at least part of the former description of respiration and the inhaling and exhaling of air refers to everyday breathing, although it is difficult to see, when inhaling, how any kind of breath (air) can rise in the spine

---

7   The same Chinese character is used when referring to both "breath" and the "mystical *Qi*."

from the lower abdomen to the shoulder blades.[8] But it is equally clear that any references to the "pre-birth to post-birth method" or "post-birth to pre-birth method" of moving *Qi* up and down the body cannot be references to breathing air, but must be alluding to that mystical force which results from concentration on external movement. The question, of course, is "What is going on here?" How can the same term, *Qi*, mean two different things? I suggest that while there is real confusion occasioned by the dual use of the term *Qi*, the relationship between the two forms of *Qi* denoted becomes at least somewhat understandable (with some of the confusion thus disappearing) when looking at the place of concentration and breathing in movement.

Movement

In the above sections we have seen that concentration and breathing are two essential elements in the practice of Taiji. Concentration is probably the most important. It entails focusing internal consciousness on external movements, linking, in the process, the mind with the body, and producing, as a result, that mystical power of *Qi*. Breathing is also important, with natural breathing being seen as the ideal. However, natural breathing is also equated with the "harmonizing" of breath, a seemingly conscious act. Furthermore, mind and breath are seen as interdependent. All of which is somewhat confusing. How can one concentrate on external movements while simultaneously trying to harmonize the breath? The conscious, focusing mind cannot do two things at once. This task becomes even more difficult when the mystical force of *Qi* is thrown into the mix. The mystical *Qi* is that force or power flowing through our bodies, a result of concentration on external movements, but also, it seems, something that we can, through purposeful willing and concentration, move up and down through our bodies. Now, if we are busy trying to concentrate on external movements so as to generate *Qi*, and at the same time we are trying to consciously harmonize our breathing, how can we possibly succeed in concentrating

---

8   Or "sink" back into the lower abdomen. However, I assume that this does not mean "air literally rises from or sinks to the lower abdomen," only something like "the physical movement of respiration—both inhaling and exhaling—starts and ends with the relaxation or tensing of the muscles of the lower abdomen, with everything in between being the route the *Qi* (breath) is imagined to take (including the movement of air into the expanding lungs between the shoulder blades)."

on the additional task of moving the *Qi* up and down our bodies? In fact, if the Taiji masters are correct, any attempt to do anything[9] except focus our internal consciousness on external movements will result in a form of Taiji that is slow, stiff, and without real power or force. How can we explain away or solve this apparent paradox or problem brought about when these different activities are all supposed to be carried out simultaneously? There seems to be only one explanation that comes close to doing so. Concentration, breathing, and movement must not be seen as separate individual activities, but as parts of a unified system, a system whose goal is a conscious and concentrated attempt at creating a harmonious synchronization of breathing and movements. There are two ways of conceiving such a system.

The first such system, which is espoused by Chen Yanling, emphasizes using breathing to lead movements (1995b, pp.1–2). Movements, in other words, are matched or coordinated with inhalations and exhalations. The ultimate goal, then, is bringing breathing and movements into exact harmony, with the Taiji practitioner consciously aware of or focused on both his/her breathing and the movements that follow it (with breathing and these movements becoming "one"). Generally speaking, this is achieved by matching movements described as insubstantial or opening with inhalations, and by matching movements described as substantial and closing with exhalations.[10] Examples include the following:

- inhaling when drawing an arm back, exhaling when extending the arm out (striking or pushing)

- inhaling when rising, exhaling when sinking

- inhaling when lifting, exhaling when lowering

- inhaling when opening up, exhaling when closing.

The speed of both the breathing and movements is determined by the individual, and at what rate of breathing he/she feels most comfortable (natural?). But one commonly accepted principle seems to be "the slower the better." Because slow breathing that you allow to drop down to the lower abdomen is said to be most effective in the generation of *Qi* and the power and good health which result from it.

---

9   Especially consciously trying to move the *Qi*.
10   See more on substantial/closing and insubstantial/opening in Chapter 3.

The second such system is at its core just the opposite of the first. Movements are not coordinated with breathing; breathing is coordinated with movements.

> ...at the appropriate time, we must use our movements to influence breathing, making breathing also become an exercise. Only then, from this complete form of exercise, can we obtain a greater impact on the health of our bodies. (Editorial Committee PPEP 1997a, p.475)

> When we practice *Taijiquan*, there are small and big movements, but our breathing must be uniform and long. It is like some people say: To match every movement perfectly with every breath, that is not possible, and not necessary. For this reason, we must only demand that in every posture, to the extent possible, we must take the insubstantial and substantial, the turns and changes, and match them to the natural cycle of breathing,[11] meaning that in every posture, we must do our utmost to find the opportunity to complete the breathing exercise given just below. When the movement of the hand is from insubstantial to substantial, our exhalation should match it using the same intention and same speed, so that when our hand has reached the end, striking out in a fist[?], at exactly that time we should exhale sufficiently, and simultaneously the lower abdomen should be tensed slightly. And, on the contrary, when the movement of the hand is from substantial to insubstantial, our inhalation should match it using the same intention and same speed, so that when our movement has stopped [and we begin a new movement], at exactly that time we inhale sufficiently, and simultaneously the lower abdomen should be relaxed. This is none other than the *Taijiquan* "Stomach Breathing Coordinated with Movements Exercise." (Editorial Committee PPEP 1997a, p.475)

Of course, in this system, what the optimum speed of both movements and breathing is, is not clear. Perhaps one starts with relatively quick movements and breathing, only gradually slowing them down.

A perfect matching of every breath with every movement is difficult. For example, sometimes, when turning or when between movements, there is need for little, if any, breathing. Still, the Forms in every style of Taiji appear to allow for a general matching of movement with

---

11 As the reader will see, the overall position espoused in this quotation seems to maintain that breathing should be matched with movements, but here the specific wording suggests that movements are to be matched with breathing. A strange inconsistency.

breathing,[12] with the apparent goal of such activity being a state of mind where one has completely let go, where one is no longer concentrating on bringing breathing and movement into harmony, but where one is, instead, absorbed in, lost in, the rhythm of the unified cycles of opening and closing in breathing and moving. Seen in this way, concentration, breathing, and movement can be understood as three elements in one rather simple system of moving meditation.

This system does not solve all the problems mentioned above that were brought about by seeing concentration, breathing, and movement as three separate elements of Taiji. It does account for the generation of the inner *Qi*. But it does not incorporate Chen Yanling's theory as concerns the "pre-birth to post-birth" and "post-birth to pre-birth" methods of circulating the inner *Qi*. Frankly, it is difficult to see how either of those methods of circulating the inner *Qi* could be incorporated into any system of moving meditation. Concentrating on the movement of the inner *Qi* would seem to necessitate turning inward, away from the sensory world, and in such a situation attempting any form of moving mediation would result in one falling over one's own feet, bumping into walls, or worse. Perhaps Chen Yanling's form of "inner Qi circulating concentration" is best attempted standing or sitting, with eyes closed.[13]

Classic Yoga[14]

The core of meditation in classic Yoga is concentration on a single point. The object of this concentration can be many things: a physical object,[15] a metaphysical thought,[16] or even God. However, this "determined

---

12 This harmony between breathing and movement definitely being easier to achieve with Yang style (or New Style) than Chen style, though.

13 Actually, the "pre-birth to post-birth" and "post-birth to pre-birth" methods of circulating the inner *Qi* remind me of the practice of Kundalini Yoga.

14 The origins of Yoga can be traced back thousands of years. Perhaps the oldest established and most revered school of Yoga is Patanjali's (fl. 2nd century BCE) Samkhya-based school of classic Yoga. There are a multitude of source materials that discuss and examine this school. However, the summary of classic Yoga presented here is based, for the most part, on just one such source—Mircea Eliade's *Yoga: Immortality and Freedom*—and the analyses it provides. Many of the ideas paraphrased here, along with the widely used and commonly accepted translations of Indian terminology, can be seen as originating in this landmark study and most excellent work on the subject. See Eliade 1969, pp.3–100.

15 For example, the tip of the nose, the space between the eyebrows, the navel, or a picture or light.

16 Such as Plato's Form of the Good.

and continuous concentration," called *ekagrata*, must be learned and practiced in stages, stages which lead from lower to higher levels of concentration. In classic Yoga these stages consist of eight different categories of exercises and techniques that are part of a "mental ascetic itinerary": restraints (*yama*), disciplines (*niyama*), bodily attitudes and postures (*asana*), regulation of respiration (*pranayama*), emancipation of sensory activity from the domination of external objects (*pratyahara*), sustained concentration (*dharana*),[17] Yogic meditation proper (*dhyana*), and total integration (*samadhi*).

Restraints

A group of self-imposed restraints is one of the necessary preliminaries for any type of asceticism, Yoga included. Five restraints in particular are advocated in classic Yoga: "not to kill" (*ahimsa*), "not to lie" (*satya*), "not to steal" (*asteya*), "sexual abstinence" (*bramacarya*), and "not to be avaricious" (*aparigraha*). These restraints are said to aim at purifying an initiate from certain sins that all systems of morality disapprove of. The practice of these restraints does not in itself result in the initiate entering any particular Yogic state. It does, however, work to help the initiate calm his/her mind and suppress what Yoga considers to be debilitating egoistic mental practices and tendencies. That makes further concentration and continued progress on the path of determined and continuous concentration possible.

Disciplines

The disciplines of Yoga, sometimes referred to as observances, are also considered one of the preliminary stages in the struggle for determined and continuous concentration. They consist of a series of bodily and psychic activities: "cleanliness" (*sauca*), or purification of the internal organs and the purging of mental evils; "serenity" (*samtosa*), especially elimination of the desire to increase the necessities of life and the turmoil that such desire brings; "asceticism" (*tapas*), bearing with the opposites of life (e.g. heat and cold); "study of self" (*svādhyāya*), including understanding the mystical syllable OM; and "contemplation of God"

---

17   The difference between *ekagrata* and *dharana* being that the latter is the sustained state of the former.

(*Īśvarapraṇidhāna*), the effort to make God (*Brahman*) the motive of all one's actions. These disciplines are also basically ethical in nature and, again like restraints, do not produce any Yogic state. They represent a continued effort to purify one's self and gain power over one's own senses by refusing to be carried along in the rushing streams of various states of consciousness.

Bodily Positions

Yoga proper begins with learning bodily attitudes and positions. Most often associated with the difficult postures of *Hatha* Yoga, these Yogic techniques aim at giving the body a stable rigidity, without physical pain or effort, during meditation. However, the practice of these postures, especially at the beginning, is anything but free of physical pain or effort. As such, they demand that the initiate suppress many of the natural efforts of his/her own body to avoid the pain—in fact, completely suspend attention to the existence of one's own body. Ultimately, the mobility of the human body is discarded, replaced by a single archetypal, iconographic posture, a posture which suggests a condition other than human. The classic lotus pose of the sitting cross-legged yogi— back straight, hands perhaps resting on knees—is the one most often associated with such a posture, but it is by no means the only one. This condition represents, through concentration, a continued mastery over the senses, but also signals the beginning of the isolation and unification of consciousness from the world of the senses.

Regulation of Respiration

One of the most important of the activities associated with Yogic postures is the regulation of respiration. This refers to the arrest of the movements of inhalation and exhalation (with respiration usually achieved through the nose). This process starts with attempts to gradually slow down the rhythm of respiration until one reaches the point where respiration is suspended as long as possible. Such a goal is usually achieved by harmonizing three movements of respiration—inhalation, retention, and exhalation—with each of these three movements occupying an equal period of time. Yogic disciplines often talk about controlling respiration as a means of penetrating the different levels of consciousness associated with different levels of breathing. They even talk of yogis who can stop their breathing indefinitely. But the real goal of regulating respiration seems to be making breathing so rhythmical that it becomes automatic, something that the yogi needs no longer to care about, and something that the yogi can abandon along with the rest of his/her body. Only in this way can the yogi then begin to fully "concentrate on a single point."

Emancipation from External Objects

Once the yogi has finished the preliminary stages of restraints and disciplines, and then moved on and mastered the physical demands of bodily positions and breathing regulation, he/she can succeed, even if only during the time practicing the exercises, in transcending the human condition. Motionless, breathing rhythmically, and with eyes and/or attention fixed on a single point, the yogi can now retreat from the sensory world into the self. At this point the yogi reaches *pratyahara*, the stage at which withdrawal of sensory activity from the domination of external objects occurs. The consciousness of the yogi has become internalized, with any connections the five senses have with external objects now broken. This is the final stage of the psycho-physiological training through which the yogi must pass if he wants to reach Truth. It allows the yogi to now move on to the final stages of determined and continuous concentration.

Final Three Stages

The final phase of Yogic meditation, called *samyama*, refers to the last three stages of determined and continuous concentration: sustained concentration, Yogic meditation proper, and total integration, a static trance-like state in which one contemplates the self.[18] These three mental states are very similar. In fact, they are so much alike that the yogi who enters one will find it difficult to stay in it, often slipping over into one of the other two. Entering the first stage means one has attained fixed consciousness on a single point. But its content is notional, implying that it realizes such a fixation of consciousness for the purpose of comprehension (being aware of itself doing so). After having achieved sustained concentration, the mind, having held itself for a period of time before itself under the form of the object of meditation, then

---

18 The term "enstasis" is often used when referring to this "contemplation of oneself."

arrives at the second stage, one that allows the yogi to penetrate into the very of essence of things. And this leads to the third and final stage—the goal, really, of all yogis who endeavor to achieve determined and continuous concentration. That is the state in which the yogi no longer uses imagination, no longer regards the act of meditation and the object of meditation as distinct from each other. Thought grasps the form of the object directly. The meditating subject, meditation itself, and the object of meditation no longer exist. Knowledge of the object of meditation and the object of knowledge are the same. All that exists, then, is the "object in itself."

Taiji vs Yoga: What Choice for You?

The short introductions to Taiji and classic Yoga given above, introductions which show Taiji and Yoga to be different in a number of ways from the many forms of both activities as commonly practiced, bring to the forefront some interesting parallels but also a good number of conspicuous differences in the central elements of these two practices—namely, concentration, breathing, and movement. Despite these differences, however, when focusing on how concentration, breathing, and movement function together, one is able to discover that both Taiji and Yoga share a fundamental dynamic which defines them as equivalent forms of meditation, a dynamic that perhaps is the essence of all forms of meditation aiming to integrate body and mind.

Concentration is the central component, the common starting point, in the practices of Taiji and Yoga. The early stages of this concentration in both forms of meditation are characterized by attempts at some kind of purification, actions that reflect the seriousness of the task at hand, but actions that also function to enhance and augment further and deeper levels of concentration. However, the kinds of purification employed in Taiji and Yoga are more different than alike. In Taiji, for example, this purification consists mostly of a relatively simple quieting and emptying of the mind, preparation for the greater concentration necessary in the activities that follow. In Yoga, on the other hand, purification is carried out both on a much wider scale and in a much more rigid and codified way. Complex physical and mental practices are introduced that aim to transform the body and the mind, paving the way, in the process, for the more difficult ascetic exercises that will follow. These practices are much more than just short preliminaries to any kind of workout or exercise routine. Instead, they should be seen as parts of a strict, almost religious regimen, one that is to be followed almost every minute of every day.[19]

Although concentration can be seen as the vehicle that helps practitioners of both Taiji and Yoga move closer to their desired goals, their goals are different. In Taiji the ultimate goal is generation of the "inner" *Qi* and the vigor, strength, longevity, focus, and peace of mind that it begets. While in classic Yoga the ultimate goal is total integration, the state of being in which a yogi experiences reality beyond the world of normal sensory experience in the "thing itself."

Breathing also plays an important role in both Taiji and classic Yoga meditation, but, again, its exact role in each system is quite different. In Taiji, breathing, like concentration, is stressed from the beginning to the end, as it provides the natural rhythm for concentration, the pattern, one might say, that helps bring together the internal and the external and their opening and closing movements. While in classic Yoga, breathing, though one means of bringing calm and order to the mind, is only a preliminary activity, something which must be mastered, and something which once mastered, like the different mental and physical restraints, disciplines, and postures, must be ignored, shoved aside, and discarded as the yogi moves to higher and more difficult planes of concentration. In addition, the breathing processes themselves differ. Yogic breathing follows a three-equal-stages pattern of inhalation, retention, and exhalation. Taiji breathing, on the other hand, based on the Principle of Opposites, has only two stages—inhalation and, when that inhalation has reached its end, a seamless move, without pause, to exhalation (then followed by a repetition of the process).

Perhaps nowhere are Taiji and Yoga more different than in the area of movement. In Taiji the focus is on movement, the inhaling and exhaling of respiration, but also the opening and closing movements of the body during the practice of Taiji Forms. In classic Yoga, on the other hand, movement is undesirable, something related to the body, something which impedes attainment of the final goal of total integration and, therefore, something that must be mastered and then discarded. This is the reason why a single, unmoving, hieratic pose is so important to yogis. It is an archetype for concentration, and reflects the resolve of the yogi as well as his/her transcendence of the human world.

---

19 Some of the masters of Taiji may have also practiced complicated systems of purification that would function as everyday "ways of living," but, generally speaking, the distinction made here holds.

Even though the differences between Taiji and classic Yoga seem to outnumber the similarities, suggesting two very unique forms of meditation, these two practices are in fact inseparably bound by a common matrix of action, something that might be referred to as the "three-part dialectic of meditation." The precise forms this "three-part dialectic of meditation" takes in Taiji and in classic Yoga do not coincide exactly, but at their core they still represent the same essential process of meditation.[20]

The practice of Taiji and classic Yoga meditation should be understood as centered on the main components as delineated in Table 2.1.

Table 2.1 Three-Part Dialectic of Meditation

Taiji	Classic Yoga
Concentrating Self	Concentrating Self
Concentration on Breathing or Movement	Awareness of Concentration
Concentration on Breathing and Movement	Awareness Only of Object of Concentration

The initial stages of both forms of meditation entail movement between each of the three components in these two groups, an oscillating interaction of sorts in which the conscious mind flitters or slides back and forth, first attempting to focus, then moving to grasp the object of its concentration, losing it, then refocusing and trying again. For example, in Taiji, the concentrating mind moves first to focus on breathing[21] while also focusing on external movements, aiming, in the process, to bring the two together as one, even though unable to do so, limited instead to focusing on one then the other, and forced always to refocus and try again and again. While in classic Yoga the concentrating mind, moving to focus on an object, first becomes aware of its concentration on the object, then pushes ahead striving only for awareness of the object, but even at these intense levels of concentration moving back and forth between its awareness of its own concentration and awareness of the object of concentration. The goal, in

---

20 Again, this is not to say that Yoga influenced (or is linked to) Taiji. This common characteristic could, of course, suggest just such a link, but it also may reflect an independent correspondence between these two different forms of meditation—something, perhaps, attributable to the nature of the human mind and how it shapes the world.

21 Following Chen Yanling's approach here and not matching breath to movement.

both Taiji and classic Yoga, is to move away from the mind just attempting to concentrate to actually achieving undistracted, unbroken, perfect focus on the object of concentration. Which is to say that in Taiji the mind is no longer just attempting to concentrate on both breathing and movements, but is actually simultaneously concentrating on breathing and concentrating on external movements. While in classic Yoga the mind moves from just attempting to concentrate on an object to becoming aware of its concentration on the object and finally only aware of the object on which it is concentrating. However, there is a paradox here. As long as the mind is striving to reach its goal, striving in Taiji to concentrate on both breathing and movements, or striving in Yoga to move beyond awareness of its concentration on an object to being only totally aware of that object, it cannot achieve its goal. The mind's ability to consciously focus on things is limited to only one such thing, and consciously striving to do it is not doing it.

At some point, then, through continued effort at concentrating, a breakthrough is somehow made (and it is this breakthrough that everyone is working towards). In Taiji, after concentrating on breathing and movement in the impossible task of trying to bring the two together, the mind leaves itself behind, and falls into the rhythm of the unified cycles of opening and closing in both breathing and moving. And in classic Yoga once sustained concentration is achieved the mind moves away from awareness of its concentration on an object, sliding over to pure concentration on or awareness of the object. In short, in both Taiji and Yoga the conscious mind, through a resolute effort at concentration, is able to break free of itself and, as a result, in Taiji generates the power of the inner *Qi*, in Yoga leads to one directly experiencing the "thing in itself"[22] (see Figures 2.1 and 2.2).

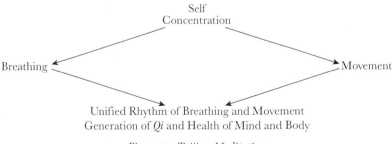

Figure 2.1 *Taiji as Meditation*

---

22 Total integration in which "the Self is the Other (*Atman* is *Brahman*)."

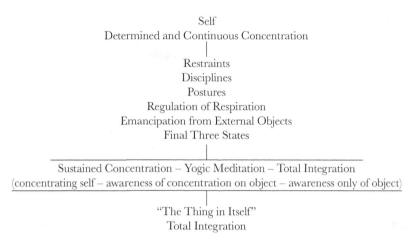

Self
Determined and Continuous Concentration

Restraints
Disciplines
Postures
Regulation of Respiration
Emancipation from External Objects
Final Three States

Sustained Concentration – Yogic Meditation – Total Integration
(concentrating self – awareness of concentration on object – awareness only of object)

"The Thing in Itself"
Total Integration

Figure 2.2 Yoga as Meditation

Taiji and Yoga as forms of meditation reflect starkly different world views that are parts of the cultures in which they developed. The Chinese world view, influenced by a "this-world" approach probably best reflected in the social philosophy of Confucianism, led to the development of a more practical regimen, one focused on natural principles like the Vital Force and the *Yin/Yang*, and one aiming at an improved physical and spiritual condition for the practitioner. The Indian world view, on the other hand, a tradition which emphasizes a reality beyond this world, is perhaps most clearly affirmed in Buddhism, in which life is seen as pain and explained within the context of the Four Pillars: *karma*, the law of universal causality, which connects human beings with the cosmos and condemns them to transmigrate indefinitely; *maya*, the cosmic illusion endured by human beings that engenders and maintains the cosmos, making indefinite transmigration necessary; *nirvana*, *atman* (the Self), or *Brahman*, the absolute reality somewhere beyond the cosmic illusion of *maya*; and Yoga, the means of gaining liberation from *maya* and attaining to real Being/Absolute Reality. The influence of both of these world views on the formation of the respective systems of meditation is clear. Taiji is anchored in this world, and the breathing and movement that are a part of it. While Yoga searches for release from this world, doing so by suppressing everyday states of consciousness.

Most people aiming to practice meditation will feel closer to one of these schools or methods over the other. Those more oriented to a truth outside our everyday world will very likely be drawn to the abstract state of absolute existence that is a part of Yoga, a state many probably often dream of, but few rarely attain. Those more oriented to this world, on the other hand, people looking to cultivate general physical and mental wellbeing, perhaps even Yoga practitioners looking for a way to enhance their own ability to concentrate while developing greater strength and health, will no doubt find themselves very comfortable with the practical regimen of Taiji, a regimen that includes concrete goals along with a set of mundane practices to achieve them.

3

Taiji Basics

For both the beginner and advanced practitioner, a systematic attempt to learn Taiji should be centered around familiarizing oneself with and practicing stances, basic steps, basic moves, and the Forms which combine them. A short warm-up, hand techniques, exercises that help one clear the mind and learn how to breathe correctly, as well as a set of essential principles one should try to incorporate into the practice of Taiji Forms, should also be learned and understood. All Taiji sessions begin with the warm-up, although this same warm-up can also be used to cool down. In addition, as the optimum time to begin learning hand techniques, correct breathing, and the essential principles of Taiji would be before practicing the basic steps and moves, in this chapter Taiji basics will be introduced in the following order:

- Warm-Up
- Basic Stances
- Hand Techniques
- Breathing Practice
- The Ten Essentials of Taiji
- Basic Steps
- Basic Moves.

Short explanations are offered for all these components, and still shots, which are taken from the videos created for this book, are provided for all except the Warm-Up.

Warm-Up

There are a variety of ways to warm up and those wishing to learn the art of Taiji are encouraged to do so in any manner they see fit or are comfortable with. However, a common routine used by Taiji practitioners consists of a short series of exercises that warms up muscles, tendons, and joints in most parts of the body in an easy and relaxed manner, starting from the wrists and ankles, then moving to the arms, back, neck, shoulders, waist, hips, knees, and finally the anterior and posterior thighs. As this routine might best be learned by watching someone else do it, readers are urged to view and follow along after the short video clip on this series of exercises (video titled Warm-Up). Some of the exercises will no doubt at first seem strange, but, as is the case with most things, practice breeds familiarity, and in very little time they should evolve into a natural part of any Taiji session.

Basic Stances

The study of Taiji begins with stances. First and foremost, stances provide the supporting frames for all the basic moves that must be learned. In fact, they create a variety of possibilities for such moves, with different stances better suited for different moves. Accordingly, strengthening one's legs is an important early part of the study of Taiji, something best accomplished, not surprisingly, by frequent practice of these same stances or the basic moves and Forms of which they are a part. This section will introduce two quasi-stances and eight regular basic stances. The quasi stances start and end all Forms, while the basic stances are used with all movements in between.

Basic stances can be broken up into three main categories that reflect their length, depth, and general level of difficulty as described in Table 3.1.

Table 3.1 Categories of Stances

Stances	Description
Small	Short stance; almost standing with only slight bending of legs and little stretching; easy.
Medium	Moderate length stance; greater bending of legs and more strenuous stretching; requiring some effort and beginning to develop real lower-body strength.
Large	Long stance; very low to ground, demanding greatest amount of strength and flexibility; creating greatest amount of stress and tension on muscles, tendons, and joints.

Large stances are usually incorporated into competition routines, with points being awarded for the level of difficulty at which the stances are performed. As a rule, then, large stances are something that the young and more athletic and advanced practitioners will probably be most interested in (although age should not be seen as a limiting factor in whether one participates in competition or not). Small stances, on the opposite end of the spectrum, are generally practiced by those who might be older, hindered by physical limitations, out of shape, or just starting their study of Taiji. Medium stances represent a moderate approach to the physical side of Taiji, and can function as the starting point for someone who is aiming at rigorous competition, or the goal for someone who is just beginning Taiji and wants to start out slowly. In order to help the greatest number of readers possible, medium stances are used in most of the still shots and videos made for this book.[1]

Stances are introduced in the relevant video (titled 2 Quasi Stances and 8 Basic Stances) in an order that allows the interested student to smoothly practice them one at a time, consecutively. It is recommended that beginners start practicing these stances first by watching and following along after the video, then by reading the descriptions attached to the still shots below. This will help them better learn their subtle nuances and differences.

---

1   Note that the category of stances one chooses will not impact the ability to correctly practice Taiji or achieve the health-giving results being pursued.

2 QUASI STANCES
Preparatory Stance and Separation Stance

1 Preparatory Stance
(1) Starts and ends all Forms. Stand upright, neck and head erect, feet parallel and close together, hands to side, palms inward, looking straight ahead.

1 → 3 Separation Stance
(2–3) From Preparatory Stance slowly pick up left foot and softly drop it to left so feet are about shoulder-width apart.

8 BASIC STANCES
1. Horse Stance

1 Separation Stance
(1) Begin in Separation Stance (or Preparatory Stance).

1 → 3 Horse Stance
(2–3) Move left foot to left so feet are double-shoulder-width apart. Sink down into a position similar to that of riding a horse, feet parallel, knees almost over feet, back straight and hands on hips.

2. 6-4 Stance (60-40 Stance)

1 Horse Stance
(1) From Horse Stance—

1 → 2 Left-Foot-Pointing 6-4 Stance
(2) Turn left foot 90 degrees to the left, pointing away from you. At the same time turn hips 45 degrees to the left, and push hips back over back right foot until body weight is distributed 60% on back right foot, 40% on front left foot. Back right knee, bent slightly, should almost be over back right foot; front left knee is also slightly bent. (Arm/hand movement to left is optional.)

2 → 3 Right-Foot-Pointing 6-4 Stance
(3) Rotate right 180 degrees, left foot pulled back in 90 degrees, right foot now pointing away from you at a 90-degree angle to the right, hips pushed back until weight is distributed 60% on back left foot, 40% on front right foot, creating a mirror image of Left-Foot-Pointing 6-4 Stance. (Arm/hand movement to right is again optional.)

3. Bow Stance

1 Right-Foot-Facing 6-4 Stance

(1) From Right-Foot-Pointing 6-4 Stance—

1 → 2 Right-Leg-Pointing Bow Stance

(2) Move front right foot to the right until right and left feet are shoulder-width apart, then sink down, moving hips forward until right knee is almost over right big toe, right foot pointing slightly inward, weight distribution 70% on front right foot, 30% on back left foot, back straight, and hips at 90-degree angles to both legs. Back left leg is straight, knee is not locked, back left toe pointing only slightly outward. Hands are dropped back to hips.

2 → 3 Left-Leg-Pointing Bow Stance

(3) Rotate left 180 degrees, creating mirror-image Bow Stance now pointing to the left, making sure to move left foot over enough so that back right and front left feet are shoulder-width apart, and sinking down and moving hips forward until left knee is almost over left big toe, left foot pointing slightly inward.

4. Golden Rooster Stance

1 Left-Leg-Pointing Bow Stance

(1) From Left-Leg-Pointing Bow Stance—

1 → 3 Left-Leg-Supported Golden Rooster Stance

(2) Move weight to right leg while pulling left leg toward you. (Left arm movement in still shot is only to create momentum.)

(3) Then move weight back to left leg, stand on it, pulling right leg up in front of until you are balancing body on left leg, left foot on ground pointing slightly outward, left knee bent slightly, right leg hanging in air, right knee at about waist or belly-button height, foot and toes of right foot relaxed and hanging down. At the same time, having taken hands off hips, bring right hand straight up directly in front of you, palm open and facing out, right arm bent at the elbow, elbow just above right knee, index finger about nose high, left arm hanging by left side, elbow bent slightly, palm facing down, parallel to the plane of the floor, just below waist height.

3 → 4 Right-Leg-Supported Golden Rooster Stance

(4) Drop right leg down to the ground, moving weight to right leg and pulling left leg up, balancing body in same way but on right leg while switching hands around and creating a mirror image of Left-Leg-Supported Golden Rooster Stance.

5. Empty Stance

1 Right-Leg-Supported Golden Rooster Stance

(1) From Right-Leg-Supported Golden Rooster Stance—

1 → 3 Left-Leg-Supported Empty Stance

(2) Drop left foot straight down and place it on the ground next to right foot at a 45-degree angle, bending knees slightly. Drop left arm/hand to side.

(3) Then pick up and extend right foot directly out in front of you, just lightly touching the toes and ball of right foot to the ground, right knee bent slightly. Weight distribution is 85% on back left foot, 15% on front right foot. At the same time, bring arms around and up in a **Raised Hands Position**, with right hand directly in front, palm open and facing out, index finger about nose height, elbow bent at a 135-degree angle, left palm open downward, index finger almost touching funny bone on right elbow. Relax both arms.

Note that in Raised Hands Position front hand always corresponds with front leg.

3 → 4 Right-Leg-Supported Empty Stance

(4) Switch legs and arms/hands around by moving right leg back, and stepping forward with left leg, while first dropping then bringing arms/hands around and up into a mirror image of the Left-Leg-Supported Empty Stance—including a now reversed Raised Hands Position.

6. Side Squat Stance

1 Right-Leg-Supported Empty Stance

(1) From Right-Leg-Supported Empty Stance—

1 → 4 Right-Leg-Supported Side Squat Stance

(2) Move hands to hips, pull left leg toward you, placing left foot next to right.

(3) Then pick up left leg, bringing knee waist high.

(4) And slide it out across the floor to left side until 70–80% of your weight is on right leg, 20–30% on left leg, right knee almost over right foot, pointing in same direction as foot, left leg straight out but left knee not tightly locked. Feet can be parallel, or toes pointing slightly outward. Keep back as straight as possible.

4 → 5 Left-Leg-Supported Side Squat Stance

(5) Reverse stance by pulling left leg toward you and dropping left foot on the floor, picking up right leg and sliding it out to the right, creating mirror image of Right-Leg-Supported Side Squat Stance.

Side Squat Stance is one of the most difficult stances for Taiji beginners, so the video and still shots show small stance examples of it. A more demanding form, the large stance, can be done by sinking down until almost squatting/sitting on main supporting foot.

7. T Stance

1 Left-Leg-Supported Side Squat Stance
(1) From Left-Leg-Supported Side Squat Stance, hands still on hips—

1 → 4 Right-Leg-Supported T Stance
(2) Pull extended right leg close to left foot, feet flat on the ground, both knees bent slightly, back straight.

(3–4) Pick up left foot and then drop it down to side, 6–8 inches from right foot, so only toes and ball of left foot are gently touching the ground. Weight distribution is about 90% on right leg, 10% on left leg.

4 → 6 Left-Leg-Supported T Stance
(5–6) Next pick up left leg, step slightly to left, putting left foot flat on floor, and pick up right foot and drop it down so only toes and ball of right foot are gently touching the ground, 6–8 inches from left foot. 90% of weight is on left leg, 10% on right, creating mirror image of Right-Leg-Supported T Stance.

Side view of Right-Leg-Supported T Stance

8. Resting Stance

1 Left-Leg-Supported T Stance

(1) In Left-Leg-Supported T Stance, hands on hips, flatten right foot against ground.

1 → 3 Left-Foot-Pointing Half Resting Stance

(2) Pick up left leg and begin to take one comfortably long step forward with left leg.

(3) Drop left foot flat on the ground, pointing toes out left at a 90-degree angle to back right foot, heels on same line, back knee almost touching ground and twisting hips to left, at which time back heel will come off the ground and weight on the back foot will rest only on the toes and ball of the back foot. Squeeze inner thighs slightly together, making sure back right knee is behind and inside front left knee, front knee slightly bent.

3 → 4 Preparatory Stance

(4) Pull left foot back, place it flat on the ground in Preparatory Stance, next to right foot.

4 → 6 Right-Foot-Pointing Half Resting Stance

(5–6) Pick up and step forward with right foot, creating mirror image of Left-Foot-Pointing Half Resting Stance.

6 → 7 Separation Stance

(7) Finished, pull right foot back next to the left into a Separation Stance and begin to drop hands from hips.

7 → 8 Preparatory Stance

(8) Then, as hands drop to sides, softly return left foot next to the right in a Preparatory Stance—ending the sequence of Basic Stances.

Half Resting Stance will be easy for most beginners. The more difficult complete Resting Stance can be achieved by sitting down on the back heel—instead of just sinking down so the knees bend slightly (complete Resting Stance is recommended only after long practice with Half Resting Stance).

HAND TECHNIQUES

When practicing Taiji the hands are generally used in simulated blocks, defensive positions (e.g. Raised Hands), grasping moves, or strikes, though in some basic moves and Forms they are also used to help with balance. There are four main shapes that the hands will take, all of which are demonstrated in the relevant video (titled Hand Techniques).

Vertical Fist

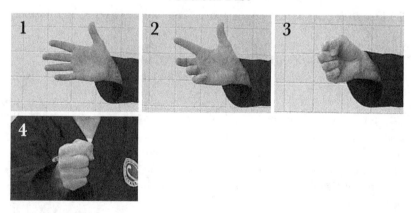

1 → 4 Vertical Fist

(1) Begin with open hand, thumb up, vertical to the floor.

(2–3) Close fist, starting with little finger and ending with thumb, squeezing tightly, thumb held snugly against middle and index fingers, fist and wrist connected as one.

(3–4) Most fist strikes occur with the knuckles of the index and middle fingers (specifically, the largest joints between those fingers and the hand), so try to keep the area between those two knuckles even with the top of the wrist.

Horizontal Fist

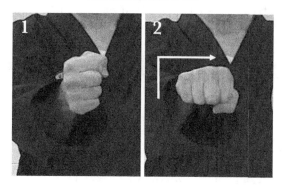

1 → 2 Horizontal Fist

(1) Begin with Vertical Fist.

(2) Turn Vertical Fist 90 degrees inward.

Again make sure knuckles are level with wrist (for some, when practicing Taiji Forms Horizontal Fist is bent upwards a little, and held loose from the wrist).

Open Palm

1 → 2 Open Palm

(1) In Separation Stance, take open hands and put them one each on corresponding buttocks, fingers pointing down.

(2) Pull hands away and up to the front, sternum high, palms out, maintaining the relaxed, semi-round, concave, inverse shape of the buttocks, with a focus in the center of the palm.

Used in defensive positions, blocks and strikes, and for balance. There are many explanations for how to make the shape of this Open Palm, but this one seems best.

Grasping Hook

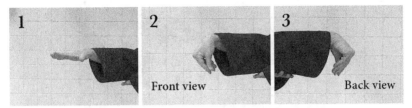

Front view   Back view

1 → 3 Grasping Hook

(1) Begin with hand open, palm facing down, parallel to the floor.

(2–3) Let wrist go limp, fingers drop down, and thumb, index, middle, and ring fingers come together as if holding the corner of a wash cloth. The little finger is resting off to the side.

Breathing Practice

As was pointed out in Chapter 2, breathing is the natural rhythm for concentration, the pattern that helps one bring together the internal and the external and their opening and closing movements. When breathing, initially pay attention to two things. First, good deep respirations start by relaxing the muscles just below the belly button and then expanding or pushing the lower abdomen out, at which time the diaphragm will move down, creating room for the lungs to expand and fill with air. Breathe the air in slowly until your lungs feel naturally full. Then begin to exhale, slowly emptying your lungs, but toward the end of the exhalation tense your stomach muscles slightly and push the stomach in as an aid to expelling any remaining air in the lungs. Second, breathe only through the nose—both inhalations and exhalations—opening your mouth just a little if your sinuses are plugged up or you become short of breath. And remember, deep, bellows-like breathing is slow, yet strong, with equal emphasis given to inhalation and exhalation, both of which are connected in a continuous and unbroken cycle of rising and falling, opening and closing.

Breathing has been incorporated into a series of simple moves—sometimes referred to as the **12 *Qigong*[2] Breathing Techniques**—which are introduced just below. These moves give new learners of Taiji the

---

2   The term *Qigong* (pronounced Chee-goong) literally means "*Qi* work" and refers to exercises that are said to help one cultivate the vital life force of Qi through breathing.

opportunity to practice and become more adept at harmonizing movements with breathing before progressing on to the basic moves and Forms. Endeavor to connect each of these moves, one with the next, in smooth, slow motions, the speeds of which are controlled by breathing. In such a way, this Breathing Practice will become one continuous routine, instead of 12 separate exercises. The relevant video (titled 12 *Qigong* Breathing Techniques), which readers are encouraged to watch before reading the descriptions below, aims to create one such routine.[3] Practice it often, any time of day, especially if you want to relieve stress and relax (although, as is the case with all Taiji activities, not immediately after eating).

12 *QIGONG* BREATHING TECHNIQUES
Opening (Preparatory Stance → Separation Stance) (2 Breaths)

(1) In Preparatory Stance slowly inhale, exhale.

(2) Then, from Preparatory Stance, slowly inhale as you pick up left leg.

(3) And exhale as you drop it down to your left into a Separation Stance.

All three steps make up Opening, the moves here being the same as those found above in Basic Stances, 2 Quasi Stances, with only breathing added.

---

3   The videos for this routine and the other moves/routines and Forms that follow, all of which should incorporate breathing, are carried out at a moderate speed—as a model, of sorts, and perhaps the starting speed for those who would like to move quickly toward deeper breathing, or the goal for those who early on feel a little faster breathing cycle is more natural. However, do remember that each practitioner can and should start at a speed that is comfortable for him/her, adjusting that speed as time passes, with the ultimate speed being one that matches what for him/her is deep, slow breathing. Everything, then, is relative to the individual practitioner.

1. Tiger Opens its Mouth (1 Breath)

1 Separation Stance
(1) From Separation Stance, hands at sides—

1 → 5 Tiger Opens its Mouth
(2) Twist hands to the outside, thumbs first, turning palms outward and upward, and as you inhale bring hands up, arms extended, in a large circular motion.

(3) Until hands reach their apex above head, fingers almost touching.

(4) Then begin to exhale and bring hands down in front of you, pushing down softly, middle fingers almost touching.

(5) Until hands reach bottom, where they relax to sides.

2. Bend Knees Palm Press (2 Breaths)

1 Separation Stance

(1) From Separation Stance, hands at sides—

1 → 5 Bend Knees Palm Press

(2) Slowly inhale as you lift outstretched arms up in front of you, shoulder-width apart, palms down and elbows slightly bent, until arms reach just about shoulder height.

(3) Then begin to exhale, bend knees and sink down, back straight and pressing down with open palms, until palms almost touch thighs. Steps **2–3** are one Bend Knees Palm Press.

(4) Return to erect Separation Stance by once again beginning to inhale as you stand up and bring hands back up to shoulder height.

(5) After which you exhale, letting arms/hands drop down in front of you and then to sides.

3. Palm Squeeze (2 Breaths)

1 Separation Stance
(1) From Separation Stance, hands at sides—

1 → 4 Palm Squeeze High
(2) Bring hands up in front of sternum, 4–6 inches apart, elbows down and in close, palms facing each other.

(3) Inhaling, separate hands until they are 12–18 inches apart.

(4) Then, exhaling, push hands back to their original position.

4 → 6 Palm Squeeze Low
(5–6) Next, drop hands down just below belly button, 4–6 inches apart, and, using the same hand actions, first inhale, separating hands (Step 5), then exhale, pushing hands closer together again (Step 6).

Finished, let arms/hands relax to sides.

The hand motions are like playing a small accordion by pulling/pushing and moving air through its bellows, the pushing motion similar to the palms squeezing something.

4. Hold the Water Barrel (1 Breath)

1 Separation Stance

(1) From Separation Stance, hands at sides—

1 → 5 Hold the Water Barrel

(2) Slowly inhale as you sink down, back straight, bending at knees, and bring open hands up in front of you around an imaginary wooden barrel filled with water that you are carrying.

Note that the "inhaling while sinking down" found in this move goes against the normal rule in Taiji of "inhaling while rising, exhaling when sinking down."

(3) Continuing without break, and still inhaling, bring hands, palms down and parallel to the plane of the floor, finger tips almost touching, close to sternum.

(4–5) Then exhale, pushing down while slowly standing up, hands settling at sides.

Exhalation and movements finish as arms/hands relax down and to sides.

5. Grab the Ball (2 Breaths)

1 Separation Stance

(1) From Separation Stance, hands at sides—

1 → 4 Grab the Ball Right

(2) Bring hands up in front of sternum about 9–12 inches apart, elbows down and in close, as if holding a soccer ball between palms.

(3) Inhaling, twist trunk and upper body to the right as many as 90 degrees, moving left hand under and right hand above the ball as you do so.

(4) Then, exhaling, return to original position.

4 → 6 Grab the Ball Left

(5) Next do the same thing to the left, except when inhaling and turning to the left, move right hand under and left hand above the ball.

(6) End by exhaling and returning to original position.

6. Cloud Hands (1 Breath)

1 Separation Stance

(1) From Separation Stance, still Grabbing the Ball in front of the sternum (5/6)—

1 → 2 Right-Facing Cloud Hands Defensive Position

(2) Begin to inhale and slide left foot along the floor out into a small or medium Right-Leg-Supported Side Squat Stance. At the same time, look to the right while rotating your right hand to the right side, palm open and facing out, index finger about nose high, right elbow bent at about a 135-degree angle, and left hand moving over and almost under right elbow, palm up, just about touching right funny bone.

2 → 4 Left-Facing Cloud Hands Defensive Position

(3–4) Smoothly, without pause, and as you begin to look 180 degrees to the left, exhale as you move hips and body weight from right leg to left leg, into a small or medium Left-Leg-Supported Side Squat Stance, while also rotating right hand down and left hand up, settling into a mirror image of Right-Facing Cloud Hands Defensive Position as exhalation ends.

All movement is in one place, with weight shifting back and forth on supporting legs, eyes following upper hand as it moves.

7. Reach and Pull (2 Breaths)

1 Left-Facing Cloud Hands Defensive Position
(1) From Left-Facing Cloud Hands Defensive Position (6/4)—

1 → 3 Right Reach and Pull
(2) Inhale and move hips and body weight from left into a Right-Leg-Supported Side Squat Stance, while at the same time rotating arms to the right, but this time reaching up to the right to about shoulder height, left hand under right, palms almost together as if grabbing something.

(3) After grabbing that something, exhale and pull it down toward your hips, beginning, as you pull, to shift hips and body weight from right leg to left leg. As hips and body weight move toward left leg and arms/hands reach the midpoint of body—

3 → 5 Left Reach and Pull
(4) Begin to inhale again and, as you settle into a Left-Leg-Supported Side Squat Stance, reach up to the left to about shoulder height, right hand under left, palms almost together as if grabbing something.

(5) Then, exhaling, pull that something down toward your hips, again shifting weight toward right leg.

This is considered two movements, both of which are cleanly broken into two equal parts—the former Steps **2–3**, the latter Steps **4–5**—and thus consists of two complete breaths.

8. Golden Rooster (2 Breaths)

1 → 2 Left-Leg-Supported Golden Rooster

(1) After completing Left Reach and Pull (7/5), body weight now having moved back to right leg and arms/hands having reached midpoint of body, reverse shifting of weight to right leg and begin to inhale again, pulling arms/hands back and moving weight toward left leg.

(2) Continue this movement back to left leg by pulling right leg up into a Left-Leg-Supported Golden Rooster Stance, complete with correct arm/hand positioning.

Reference 8 Basic Stances, #4, Golden Rooster, for more help with correct arm/hand positioning.

2 → 4 Right-Leg-Supported Golden Rooster

(3) Then, as you begin to exhale, drop right leg and right arm/hand down toward the ground.

(4) After right foot touches ground, smoothly and without pause begin new inhalation, bringing left leg up into a Right-Leg-Supported Golden Rooster Stance, complete with mirror-image arm/hand positioning.

4 → 5 Preparatory Stance/Separation Stance

(5) Once Right-Leg-Supported Golden Rooster Stance is complete, exhale and drop left leg and left arm/hand down into a Preparatory or Separation Stance, arms/hands relaxing at sides.

9. Bow Stance Push (2 Breaths)

1 Preparatory Stance/Separation Stance

(1) From Preparatory or Separation Stance (8/5)—

1 → 4 Right-Leg-Pointing Bow Stance Push

(2) Step out in front of you into a Right-Leg-Pointing Bow Stance, arms extended straight out at about shoulder height, a little less than shoulder-width apart, elbows bent slightly, palms facing down.

(3) From Bow Stance, inhale and rock back, moving weight to front right heel and back left leg, hands pulled back, palms open, ready to push.

(4) Then exhale and push forward with two open palms, returning to original Right-Leg-Pointing Bow Stance, and ending with arms extended as in Step 2.

4 → 6 Left-Leg-Pointing Bow Stance Push

(5–6) Done, switch to a Left-Leg-Pointing Bow Stance, arms extended, and repeat rocking and pushing motions in Steps 3–4, including correct breathing.

After second Bow Stance Push, return to Separation Stance.

Each rocking and pushing movement is completed in one breath.

10. Inside, Down and Up (2 Breaths)

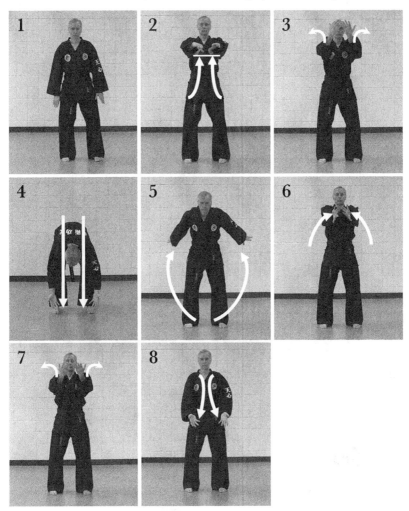

1 Separation Stance

(1) From Separation Stance after Left-Leg-Pointing Bow Stance Push (after 9/6)—

1 → 8 Inside, Down, and Up

(2) Inhale, bring arms/hands up in front of you until almost at shoulder height, a little less than shoulder-width apart, elbows bent slightly, palms facing down.

(3) Then twist hands outward, thumbs first, turning palms up.

(4) And, while exhaling, bend forward at waist, reaching down until you can touch (or get close to touching) the ground with the back tips of middle fingers.

(5) From there, beginning to inhale again, roll arms out and around as you stand.

(6) Until, as you stand erect, arms are extended straight out in front of you again, this time hands almost touching back to back.

(7) Then, starting to exhale, turn palms so they are again facing up.

(8) And, continuing to exhale, slowly drop hands down and then to side, still in Separation Stance.

This is considered two movements and thus incorporates two breaths.

11. Outside, Down and Up (2 Breaths)

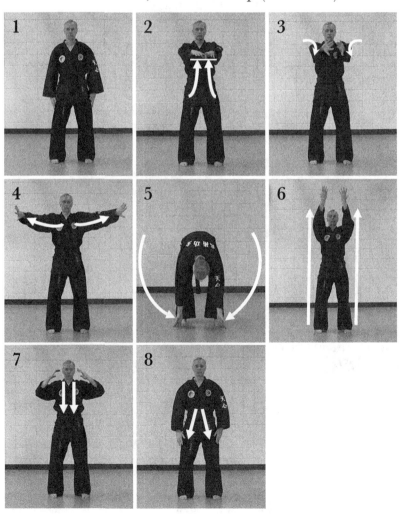

1 Separation Stance

(1) From Separation Stance at end of 10/8—

1 → 8 Inside, Down, and Up

(2) Inhale, bring arms/hands up in front of you until almost at shoulder height, a little less than shoulder-width apart, elbows bent slightly, palms facing down.

(3) Then, continuing to inhale, twist hands, thumbs first, inward, turning palms outward.

(4) And roll arms out and around in a large circular breaststroke-like swimming motion.

(5) When arms are fully extended at sides, exhale and bend forward at waist, reaching down until you can touch (or get close to touching) the ground with the front tips of middle fingers.

(6) From there, begin to inhale again, bringing arms/hands, shoulder-width apart, straight up in front and above your head.

(7) Then, turning palms down, begin to exhale as you slowly push down with palms, down past the outsides of the ears.

(8) Until you are done pushing and arms/hands are at sides, exhalation now complete, still in Separation Stance.

This is considered two movements and thus incorporates two breaths.

12. Cross Arms (1 Breath)

1 Separation Stance

(1) From Separation Stance of 11/8—

1 → 6 Cross Arms

(2) Inhale and bring hanging arms/hands together, close to front of body, just below sternum, until they touch at the wrists, palms inward, left hand inside right.

(3) Then, still inhaling, arms crossed and wrists still touching, bring arms/hands straight up, turning wrists, until arms/hands are above your head (right hand now inside left).

(4) From there, rotate wrists so that palms face outward, still standing erect.

(5) Then begin to exhale, extending arms/hands around in a large outward circular motion.

(6) Until arms/hands come together again just below belly button, right hand inside left, left hand resting on right wrist.

Closing (Separation Stance → Preparatory Stance) (1 Breath)

(1) From Separation Stance at end of Cross Arms (12/6)—

(2) Slowly inhale as you pick up left leg, then exhale as you drop it next to right leg in Preparatory Stance.

(3) Finally, let hands fall from belly-button area to relax at sides (hand movements to sides may also accompany leg movement in Step 2, thus completing Steps 2–3 in one movement instead of two, all with one breath).

Closing marks the end of Breathing Practice and the 12 *Qigong* Breathing Techniques. Closing also functions to end routines and Forms in Taiji. Closing is the reversal of movements found in the Opening of 12 *Qigong* Breathing Techniques.

Ten Essential Principles of Taiji

Taiji is generally broken into three overlapping stages: practicing how to carry one's body (stances, steps, and postures), mastering how to synchronize and harmonize breathing with movements, and learning the correct state of mind. To help beginner and intermediate practitioners organize and more easily remember the different ideas, techniques, and practices in these stages, a system of guidelines considered most vital to correctly learning Taiji has been formulated.[4] This system, which consists of ten general principles, serves as a list of easy-to-remember checkpoints that are especially helpful when practicing basic moves and the Forms of which they are a part.

---

4   Attributed to Yang Chengfu (1997b, pp.314–5). Another English version of these Essentials can be seen at www.itcca.it/peterlim/ycf10pts.htm.

1. **Relax neck, straighten head.** Stand in an upright stance, holding the head and neck naturally erect. Do not strain or otherwise push the head up unnaturally.

2. **Hold chest in, keep back erect.** By keeping the head and neck erect, the chest will be naturally pulled in, the spine naturally elongated.

3. **Lower shoulders, drop elbows.** Release the energy and tenseness from your shoulders. Do not consciously raise your elbows.

4. **Loosen waist.** The waist area, the center of gravity, is the starting point for all movement, the lower belly the beginning point of breathing. A tight waist will work to impede all movement and result in stiff and clumsy technique.

5. **Stress intent, not strength.** This is often interpreted to mean "Use the mind instead of force." How can one use the mind? When practicing Forms, do not emphasize any one part of the body or exert force in any one particular movement; just relax the whole body and let go, simply concentrating on your breathing and movements and allowing the body to take over. (See Chapter 2 above.)

6. **Link movements without pause.** In Taiji there are no separate movements, only a continuous flow of movements done slowly and smoothly, without pause, from one to the next, from the beginning of a Form to its end.

7. **Harmonize the internal and external.** Taiji entails concentrating on both your internal breathing and external movements, while endeavoring to synchronize or harmonize them in a common cycle of opening and closing. (See Chapter 2 above.)

8. **Upper and lower move as one.** The internal and external form a harmonious cycle of opening and closing, the upper body and lower body forming a unified whole. As the feet move, so do the waist, trunk, arms, and head also respond and follow, forming a connected and coordinated whole.

9. **Make explicit the empty and full.** Movement in Taiji is based on the Principle of Opposites, a reflection of *Yin/Yang* philosophy, with the *Yin* associated with the empty/insubstantial, the *Yang* the full/substantial. This can be better understood by looking

at stances. Weight distribution in most stances is rarely evenly balanced. In the Bow Stance, for example, 70% of the weight is on the front leg, 30% on the back, with the front leg thus said to be full/substantial, the back leg empty/insubstantial. However, just as the *Yin* and *Yang* are said to wax and wane with the seasons, the *Yin* growing in strength as winter approaches, the *Yang* flourishing from spring to summer, so too in moving within and between stances can one see the changing cycles of these two forces. For example, as will be explained below with steps and basic moves, when moving forward from a Left-Leg Pointing Bow Stance, one first rocks back, transferring the weight from the front left leg (which becomes empty/insubstantial) to the back right leg (making it full/substantial). Then, as one moves the back right leg ahead by stepping forward, one again transfers the weight to the front left-supporting leg (making it now full/substantial again and the back leg empty/insubstantial), before stepping out on to the right leg (transferring the weight to the right leg and making it full/substantial) and completing what is called **Front Step**. During this whole process, weight shifts back and forth from one leg to another, creating cycles in which the full/substantial and empty/insubstantial are constantly changing. As steps become more natural and spontaneous, other movements are also added— rising/sinking, blocking/striking, etc.—with all of them patterned on this complementary cycle of opposites and coordinated in a manner that harmonizes them with internal breathing.

10. **In movement seek stillness.** Empty the mind of all distracting thoughts and feelings and quietly focus on internal breathing and external movements. Only then can one begin to make progress in synchronizing and harmonizing breathing and movement in the common cycle of opening and closing.

3 BASIC STEPS

Basic steps demonstrate the three main directions in which one will usually move when practicing the basic moves or Forms of Taiji— forward, backward, and sideways. By changing the angle of one's movement one can also use these steps, especially the forward and backward steps, to move diagonally. When learning basic steps, beginners should start trying to incorporate breathing into their movements and, as they become more adept at these steps, focus on using the respiration cycle to control the speed of movements while attempting to bring breathing and movement together as one. **Carry the Water Barrel**, which is introduced below following the 3 Basic Steps, is a good way to focus on such control. In addition, in all movements of these steps pay especially close attention to the shifting of weight from one leg to the other as explained in the Ten Essential Principles of Taiji, #9. Multiple still shots and descriptions of each step are provided below, although readers are encouraged to first watch the pertinent video (titled 3 Basic Steps and Carry the Water Barrel) when learning these moves.

1. Front Step

1 → 2 Opening (2 Breaths)

(1–2) Do Opening, making sure to breathe correctly, and ending in Separation Stance.

Reference 12 *Qigong* Breathing Techniques, Opening, for help with coordinating movements and breathing.

2 → 5 Left-Leg Front Step (1 Breath)

(3) From Separation Stance, put hands behind hips, inhaling as you drag left leg toward right leg in a **Semi-T Stance** and begin to turn to left.

(4–5) Without pause, exhale and step left 90 degrees, first on to left heel, then on to whole left foot, ending in Left-Leg-Pointing Bow Stance.

5 → 8 Right-Leg Front Step (1 Breath)

(6) Inhaling again, rock back, moving weight to back right foot and elevating all but heel of left front foot off the floor, turning left front ankle and foot to the outside as you do.

(7) Then, still inhaling, step forward until back right foot begins to pass front left leg.

(8) At which time begin to exhale and complete step forward by moving into a Right-Leg-Pointing Bow Stance, again, heel first, then on to complete foot.

Repeat this Front Step several times as you alternate legs in moving forward, paying attention to the slow shifts in weight from one leg to the other, from the full to the empty and back again, stopping in a Left-Leg-Pointing Bow Stance.

Reference Ten Essential Principles of Taiji, #9, for help remembering the full and empty.

Note that each Front Step forward is achieved with one complete cycle of respiration (one inhalation, one exhalation).

2. Back Step

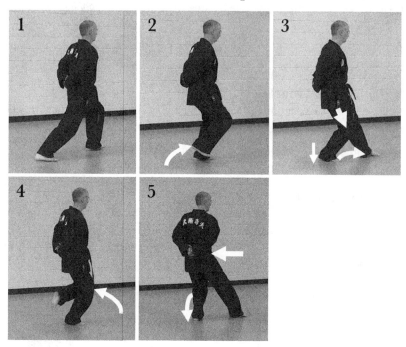

1 Left-Leg-Pointing Bow Stance

(1) From Left-Leg-Pointing Bow Stance (after Front Step 8), hands still behind hips—

1 → 3 Right-Leg-Supported Empty Stance (1 Breath)

(2) Slowly inhale, bringing back right foot up just behind front left foot.

(3) And as you exhale, step out with front left foot into a Right-Leg-Supported Empty Stance.

3 → 5 Left-Leg Back Step (1 Breath)

(4) From this Right-Leg-Supported Empty Stance, begin to slowly inhale, picking up front left foot and stepping back into another Empty Stance. However, halfway through stepping back, as front foot moves back just past body, begin to exhale.

(5) Complete the exhalation as you step into a Left-Leg-Supported Empty Stance.

Repeating Steps 3–5 with the opposite right leg would be a **Right-Leg Back Step**.

Repeat this Back Step several times, alternating legs as you go and paying attention to the slow shifts in weight from one leg to another, stopping in a Right-Leg-Supported Empty Stance.

Note that the movements from Bow Stance to Empty Stance (Steps **1–3**) and each Back Step are all achieved with one complete cycle of respiration (one inhalation, one exhalation).

3. Side Step

1 Right-Leg-Supported Empty Stance

(1) From Right-Leg-Supported Empty Stance (after Back Step 5), hands still behind hips—

1 → 2 Separation Stance

(2) Turn body to the right 90 degrees and pull front left leg back into Separation Stance, knees slightly bent.

2 → 5 Left-Leg Side Step (1 Breath)

(3) From this knees-bent Separation Stance, inhale and slide left foot along the floor and out into a Right-Leg-Supported Side Squat Stance.

(4) Then, without pause, begin to move weight from the right leg to the left, pushing hips to the left, and halfway through this movement beginning to exhale.

(5) Finally, as you finish exhalation started in Step 4, drag the right leg along after the hips, moving into another knees-bent Separation Stance.

This may seem like a three-stage step: sliding left foot to the left, moving hips in same direction following the left foot, and dragging right foot after hips. But when matching the movements to breathing, it turns into a two-stage move: inhale as you slide left foot to the left, continue to inhale as you begin to move hips left after the left foot, but halfway through moving the hips left begin to exhale, completing the hip movement left and finishing the exhalation as you drag right foot into another Separation Stance.

Repeat Left-Leg Side Step several times.

5 → 8 Right-Leg Side Step (1 Breath)

(6) Then, stopping in Separation Stance (Step 5), reverse direction, and slide right foot out.

(7) Moving the hips after it.

(8) And dragging left foot into a new Separation Stance—all in one respiration, concentrating on the rhythmical shifting of weight from leg to leg as you move and breathe.

Repeat Right-Leg Side Step in that opposite direction several times, stopping in a Separation Stance.

Carry the Water Barrel

1 Separation Stance

(1) Still in Separation Stance (after Side Step 8), hands behind back, knees slightly bent—

1 → 5 Carry the Water Barrel (1 Breath Each)

(2–3) Inhale as, bending knees a little more, you sink down and Hold the Water Barrel, at the same time beginning to turn 90 degrees to your left and dragging left leg toward right leg into a Semi-T Stance.

(4) Then exhale and, completing 90-degree turn left, take a Left-Leg Front Step that ends in a Left-Leg-Pointing Bow Stance.

(5) Follow this with a Right-Leg Front Step into a Right-Leg-Pointing Bow Stance, rocking first to the rear, then moving forward, breathing appropriately.

All the while you are moving, hold the imaginary water barrel. As it is "full of water," move slowly, without rocking up and down, so as not to "spill" the water.

Repeat Front Steps several times as you alternate legs in moving forward, paying attention to the slow shifts in weight from one leg to the other, to the heel then to the complete foot, all while breathing correctly.

Also note that each Front Step is achieved with one complete cycle of respiration, with respiration controlling the shifting of weight.

If necessary, reference 3 Basic Steps, #1, Front Step, for more details on coordinating step movement, transfer of weight, and breathing.

6 → 9 Right Twist Step (1 Breath)

(6) When turning around, start from a Left-Leg-Pointing Bow Stance.

(7) As you inhale, rock back on front left heel, turning left foot inward 90 degrees, back foot outward slightly, and moving weight from front left foot to back right foot, as you begin to turn body 180 degrees right.

(8) Then, without pause, move weight back to left foot as you drag the right foot back in front of it in a Semi-T Stance.

(9) 180-degree turn finished, exhale, stepping to your rear, first on to right heel, then on to right foot, completing a Right-Leg-Pointing Front Step.

Steps 7–9 are the Right Twist Step.

Continue ahead using Front Steps, still Carrying the Water Barrel, alternating legs and paying attention to slow shifting of weight as you breathe.

9 → 11 Return and Closing (1 Breath)

(10) Stop in a Right-Leg-Pointing Bow Stance (like Step 9), and begin to inhale as you move weight to back left leg, turning right foot inward 90 degrees.

(11) Then as you move weight back to right leg and drag left leg into a knees-bent Separation Stance, exhale and stand, pushing down with palms as you do so until hands are at side.

Steps **9–11** can be called a **Half Left-Leg Return**. Compare below with 8 Postures, #8, Return and Closing, Steps **2–5**.

From Separation Stance, hands at side, end Carry the Water Barrel with Closing. Reference 12 *Qigong* Breathing Techniques, Closing, if you still need more details on this ending.

12 BASIC MOVES

The 12 Basic Moves of Taiji are martial arts techniques, each of which has a number of different situational applications. Knowing how such moves could be applied in a sparring or fighting situation, therefore, would help one to learn them more easily. However, as the focus of this book is Taiji as moving meditation, and teaching martial applications would detract from this focus, only passing references are made to some simple blocks, kicks, punches, and other moves.[5] Emphasis is instead placed on helping learners concentrate on developing the rhythmical coordination of breathing and movement that is the core dynamic of Taiji.

The 12 Basic Moves can be seen as formed in a cumulative, building-blocks manner by combining stances, steps, hand and leg techniques, and steady, rhythmical breathing. As such, learning these basic moves is made easier if one regularly looks back and reviews the 8 Basic Stances, 12 *Qigong* Breathing Techniques, and 3 Basic Steps. In fact, it is assumed the reader will do just that,[6] although from time to time references will also be made back to things already learned. In addition, where new techniques are added—especially blocks, strikes, and kicks—new details will be added that help the reader incorporate those techniques correctly into the cycles of breathing and movement that make up the 12 Basic Moves.

---

5   In fact, exactly what the martial applications of some Taiji moves are is not clear. Those introduced in this book are relatively simple interpretations, given as aids to help readers learn the different moves as part of Taiji as moving meditation. Readers perhaps interested in more complex situational (sparring) applications might want to reference works like Shou-Yu Liang and Wen-Ching Wu's *Tai Chi Chuan: 24 and 48 Postures With Martial Applications* (Roslindale, MA: YMAA, 1996).

6   Just as in the next chapter it will be assumed the beginner is looking back and reviewing and practicing the 12 Basic Moves when learning the Forms that they make up.

Again, readers are encouraged to first watch and perhaps follow along with the relevant video (titled 12 Basic Moves), then read these explanations, as the explanations should help them better understand some of the subtle nuances of the 12 Basic Moves, especially how to breathe correctly.[7] These 12 Basic Moves can be repeated any number of times within the routine that they constitute, though the video shows them performed in sequences of two or three moves each, coordinated as such to make it easier to shift from one move to the next, thus creating an easy-to-follow series.

Opening
1. Part the Wild Horse's Mane

---

7   The opening and closing of external movements should be coordinated with internal breathing, and practitioners are encouraged to do just this, though they might want to adjust things somewhat if they can find more "natural" ways better suited to their own practice.

1 Separation Stance

(1) From Separation Stance, hands hanging at sides—

1 → 3 Bend Knees Palm Press (1 Breath)

(2) Lift outstretched arms up in front of you, palms down and elbows slightly bent, until arms reach just about shoulder height.

(3) Then, exhaling, sink down, completing Bend Knees Palm Press.

Reference 12 *Qigong* Breathing Techniques, #2, Bend Knees Palm Press, for further help with coordination of movements and breathing.

3 → 5 Left-Hand Part the Mane (1 Breath)

(4) As you complete Bend Knees Palm Press, inhaling, and turning slightly left, pull left leg in next to right leg in a Semi-T Stance, and Grab the Ball, left hand under right.

(5) Then exhale as you take Left-Leg Front Step 90 degrees to left, striking with upper edge of left hand and pulling right hand back and down to side where it rests, parallel to the plane of the floor. Striking motion with left hand and Front Step should both be completed at the same time—as exhalation ends.

5 → 10 Right-Hand and Left-Hand Part the Mane (2 Breaths)

(6–7) Following the pattern of multiple Front Steps, and starting from Left-Leg-Pointing Bow Stance (Step 5), inhale and rock back in place, turning left foot to the outside, then, stepping forward, Grab the Ball again, this time right hand under left, as you begin Right-Leg Front Step.

(8) Exhale as you finish Right-Leg Front Step, striking with the upper edge of right hand and pulling left hand back and down to your side.

(9–10) Do one more Left-Hand Part the Wild Horse's Mane, first inhaling and then following the pattern of rocking back, stepping forward while Grabbing the Ball, now left hand under right, and ending in a Left-Leg-Pointing Bow Stance and left-hand strike.

As with Front Step, each Part the Wild Horse's Mane consists of one complete respiration in which the focus is on the rhythmical shifting of weight from one leg to the next, while adding hand strike and slowly breathing.

Reference 3 Basic Steps, #1, Front Step, for more details on coordinating step movement, transfer of weight, and breathing.

2. Roll Away Forearm (Repulse Monkey)

1 Left-Hand Part the Mane

(1) From the Left-Leg-Pointing Bow Stance in Left-Hand Part the Wild Horse's Mane (1/10)—

1 → 2 Empty Stance and Crescent Hands (½ Breath)

(2) Inhaling, move to Empty Stance, all while opening arms into **Crescent Hands Position** by turning front left palm, directly in front now, upwards slightly, index finger about nose height, arm bent at about a 135-degree angle, and by bringing right hand up, at about a 45-degree angle to the rear, index finger about ear height, palm up, arm bent at about a 135-degree angle.

Reference 3 Basic Steps, #2, Back Step, Steps 2–3, for details on movement to Empty Stance, noting that the full breath in Steps 2–3 there is only an inhalation here.

2 → 5 Right-Hand Repulse Monkey (½ Breath)

(3–4) Then, as you begin Left-Leg Back Step, slowly exhale, following with your eyes the back right hand as you move it forward with a chest-high **Right-Hand Palm Thrust**, the front left hand being simultaneously pulled back toward body. The two palms should almost touch in passing, right above left.

(5) Exhalation ends in a Left-Leg-Supported Empty Stance, left hand resting by left hip, palm up, right hand, having completed Palm Thrust, now positioned directly in front, index finger about chest height, palm facing out, arm slightly bent.

Steps 2–5 as described here entail one complete respiration (though one could make it two).

5 → 8 Left-Hand Repulse Monkey (1 Breath)

(6) After Right-Hand Repulse Monkey, without pause, begin mirror-image move by first inhaling as you move arms/hands to new Crescent Hands Position, arms reversed.

(7–8) Then, starting Right-Leg Back Step, slowly begin to exhale and complete Right-Leg Back Step by moving into a Right-Leg-Supported Empty Stance, at the same time completing chest-high **Left-Hand Palm Thrust** with back hand, right hand ending by right hip, palm up.

Make sure to pay attention to the slow shifts in weight from one leg to another as you breathe and move, if necessary referencing 3 Basic Steps, #2, Back Step.

3. Brush Knee (Stepping Forward)

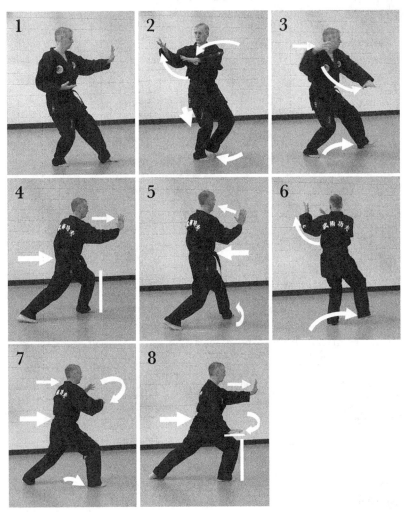

1 Left-Hand Repulse Monkey

(1) From Right-Leg-Supported Empty Stance in Left-Hand Repulse Monkey (2/8)—

1 → 4 Left-Right-Hands Brush Knee (1 Breath)

(2) Slowly inhale as you drag front left foot back toward right foot into a Semi-T Stance, at the same time moving right hand up, at about a 45-degree angle to the rear, index finger about ear height, palm up, and arm bent at a 135-degree angle, while bringing left hand over the top in a semi-circular motion until almost touching right elbow. This is called **Left-Right-Hands Brush Knee Strike Ready Position**.

(3–4) Then begin to exhale, reversing direction, and take Left-Leg Front Step into a Left-Leg-Pointing Bow Stance, brushing away (blocking) an opponent's knee (kick) to your left with left hand while striking that opponent in solar plexus area with Right-Hand Palm Thrust. Left hand stops at left side, just below hip height, parallel to the plane of the floor.

4 → 8 Right-Left-Hands Brush Knee (1 Breath)

(5–6) Next, begin new mirror-image move by inhaling and first rocking back, then starting Right-Leg Front Step while reversing arm movements in Step 2, creating a **Right-Left-Hands Brush Knee Strike Ready Position**.

(7–8) Which ends while exhaling and moving into a Right-Leg-Pointing Bow Stance, brushing away (blocking) an opponent's knee (kick) to your right with right hand while striking that opponent in solar plexus area with Left-Hand Palm Thrust. Right hand stops at right side, just below hip height, parallel to the plane of the floor.

Exhalations end when Bow Stances are complete and you have finished Brush Knee and Palm Thrust movements.

4. Heel Kick

1 Right-Left-Hands Brush Knee
(1) From Right-Leg-Pointing Bow Stance at end of Right-Left-Hands Brush Knee (3/8)—

1 → 4 Left Twist Step (1 Breath)
(2–3) Slowly inhale as you rock back and move weight to back left leg, bringing arms together in toward body, wrist to wrist, palms facing body, right arm inside left. Then circle hands above head and outwards and, beginning to exhale, start moving weight back to right leg.

(4) Continuing to exhale, turn to the rear and finish moving weight back to right leg as you drag left leg close to the right leg in a Semi-T Stance and drop arms/hands down in front of body, wrist to wrist, palms toward body, left (kicking side) hand outside (beginning of Cross Arms).

4 → 6 Left-Foot Heel Kick (1 Breath)

(5) Without pause, inhaling, pull left leg up, knee pointing slightly out, into Right-Leg-Supported Golden Rooster Stance, arms/hands continuing Cross Arms movement and coming up, but stopping sternum high.

(6) From Right-Leg-Supported Golden Rooster Stance, exhale as you extend left leg out into a Heel Kick, left toes pulled back tightly, knee locking for a second, arms/hands also coming up and around in an outside circular motion until left arm hangs parallel to and above left leg, index finger about nose height, palm out, elbow slightly bent, and right arm settles at about a 45-degree angle to the rear, index finger about ear height, palm out, and arm bent at a 135-degree angle.

Arm placement is called **Balance Position**.

6 → 9 Right-Foot Heel Kick (1 Breath)

(7) Exhalation and kick completed, step forward by dropping left kicking leg down on to left foot.

(8) Then, as you inhale, bring right leg up into a Left-Leg-Supported Golden Rooster Stance, legs and arms in mirror positions to Step 5.

(9) Followed by another exhalation as you extend right leg out into a Heel Kick, arms/hands in reversed Balance Position.

5. Cloud Hands

1 Right-Foot Heel Kick
(1) From Right-Foot Heel Kick (4/9)—

1 → 6 Two Left-Moving Cloud Hands (2 Breaths)
(2) Slowly inhale as you drop right leg down into a Right-Facing Cloud Hands Defensive Position (with small or medium Right-Leg-Supported Side Squat Stance)—really the first half of Left-Leg Side Step.

(3–4) As you then begin to exhale, complete Left-Leg Side Step, dragging right leg and moving hips left into a Separation Stance, complete with hand placement in Left-Facing Cloud Hands Defensive Position.

Eyes are always following upper rotating hand, and attention paid to breathing and shifting of weight from one leg to the other as the arms/hands rotate.

(5) From Separation Stance, inhaling, begin Left-Leg Side Step again, sliding left foot left along the floor into a small or medium Right-Leg-Supported Side Squat Stance with hands in Right-Facing Cloud Hands Defensive Position.

(6) Then, without pause, as you exhale, complete Left-Leg Side Step, dragging right leg and moving hips into Separation Stance complete with hand placement in Left-Facing Cloud Hands Defensive Position.

Steps 2–6 are two examples of Left-Moving Cloud Hands. From the Separation Stance in Step 6, reversing the direction and creating mirror-image moves to the right would be **Right-Moving Cloud Hands**.

6. Grasp the Swallow's Tail

1 Left-Facing Cloud Hands Defensive Position
(1) From the Separation Stance in Left-Facing Cloud Hands Defensive Position
(5/6)—

1 → 2 Half Left-Moving Cloud Hands (½ Breath)
(2) Begin another Left-Moving Cloud Hands, inhaling and sliding left leg out
to the left while moving into a Right-Facing Cloud Hands Defensive Position.

2 → 13 Right Grasp the Swallow's Tail (2½ Breaths)

(3–4) But then, instead of completing Left-Leg Side Step by dragging right leg and moving hips into a Separation Stance complete with hand placement in Left-Facing Cloud Hands Defensive Position, still looking to the right, continue inhaling as you drag right leg up close to the left leg in a Semi-T Stance, and Grab the Ball, right hand under left (the beginning of a Right-Leg Front Step to the right).

(5–6) Then, without pause, begin to exhale and move into Right-Leg Front Step, striking opponent in solar plexus area with back of right hand (called **Right-Arm Ward Off**), at the same time pulling and dropping left hand to left side, just below hip, palm down and parallel to the plane of the floor.

(7) From Right-Leg Pointing Bow Stance and Right-Arm Ward Off position, inhaling, reach forward, grabbing opponent's arm, left hand under right.

(8) And pull opponent back and to your left side (called **Pull Back**), keeping front foot flat on floor, and turning hips to the left slightly.

(9–10) Then, exhaling, shove opponent away with back of right hand/wrist/arm (called **Press**), left open hand up against inside of right wrist, arms finishing in front in a half-circle shape.

(11–13) From Press, still in a Right-Leg-Pointing Bow Stance (Step 10), carry out a Bow Stance Push, making sure to coordinate breathing with rocking and push.

13 → 21 Left Grasp the Swallow's Tail (3 Breaths)

(14–21) Moving ahead from the Right-Leg Pointing Bow Stance in Step 13, do a mirror-image Grasp the Swallow's Tail starting with a Left-Leg Front Step, complete with rocking back and Grab the Ball, left hand under right, followed by a **Left-Arm Ward Off**, then a Pull Back, Press, and Bow Stance Push, all ending in Left-Leg Pointing Bow Stance.

Do another Grasp the Swallow's Tail, this one a Right Grasp the Swallow's Tail, ending in a Right-Leg Pointing Bow Stance (3 Breaths).

Note that any one Grasp the Swallow's Tail is completed in three complete respirations.

7. Overhead Block and Palm Thrust

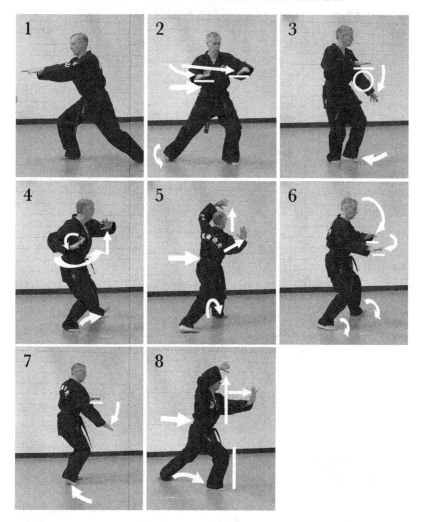

1 Bow Stance Push of Right Grasp the Swallow's Tail (End)

(1) From a Right-Leg-Pointing Bow Stance, arms still extended after ending Bow Stance Push of Right Grasp the Swallow's Tail (after **6/21**)—

1 → 3 Left Twist Step (½ Breath)

(2) Slowly inhale and rock back, moving weight to back left leg as you pull right foot in 90 degrees and begin to turn body 225 degrees to the left in a wide Left Twist Step.

(3) Still inhaling, move weight back to right leg and pull left leg in close to the right leg in a Semi-T Stance, Grabbing the Ball, left hand under right.

3 → 5 Left Overhead Block and Right Palm Strike (½ Breath)

(4–5) Next, exhale, completing 225-degree turn and stepping out into a Left-Leg-Pointing (Slanted) Bow Stance, protecting head with an overhead **Left-Hand Palm Block** while striking your opponent in solar plexus area with a Right-Hand Palm Thrust.

5 → 8 Right Overhead Block and Left Palm Strike (1 Breath)

(6–8) Without pause, rotate feet and turn 90 degrees to the right, carrying out a mirror-image Overhead Block and Palm Thrust—inhaling as you first move weight to back right leg, then to left leg as you pull right leg in close to left leg in a Semi-T Stance, and Grab the Ball, right hand under left. Then, exhaling, step into a Right-Leg Pointing (Slanted) Bow Stance, protecting head with an overhead **Right-Hand Palm Block** and striking with a Left-Hand Palm Thrust. Concentrate on inhalations and exhalations while shifting weight from leg to leg and moving arms and palms to block and strike.

8. Hammer Fist Block to Pull and Shove

1 Right-Left Overhead Block and Palm Thrust

(1) From a Right-Leg-Pointing (Slanted) Bow Stance, arms/hands still in Right-Left Overhead Block and Palm Thrust (7/8)—

1 → 3 Left Twist Step (½ Breath)

(2) Begin a wide Left Twist Step, slowly inhaling and rocking back, moving weight to back left leg, and pulling right foot in 90 degrees, as body starts to turn 270 degrees to the left.

(3) Still inhaling, move weight back to right leg and pull left leg in close to the right leg in a Semi-T Stance while dropping left hand/fist down under right hand, which is parallel to the plane of the floor.

3 → 5 Left Hammer Fist Block (½ Breath)

(4–5) Then, exhaling and completing 270-degree turn, step out into a Left-Leg-Pointing (Slanted) Bow Stance, bringing left fist up inside right arm, around and then down in a Hammer Fist Block, fist stopping just about shoulder height, arm directly above left leg, elbow bent about 90 degrees, and the index finger of the right hand, palm down and fingers extended, just about touching the left elbow funny bone. Exhalation ends as you step into Bow Stance and complete Hammer Fist Block.

5 → 9 Right Pull and Shove (1 Breath)

(6) Next, as you inhale, rock back, moving weight to front left heel and back right foot, while turning 90 degrees to the right and reaching over to grab your opponent, left hand under right.

(7) After which, still inhaling, pull opponent toward you as you drag right leg over next to the left leg in a Semi-T Stance.

(8–9) Then, exhaling, step out into a Right-Leg-Pointing (Slanted) Bow Stance, shoving opponent away with a Press.

9 → 13 Left Pull and Shove (1 Breath)

(10) Repeat this Pull and Shove move to the left with mirror-image moves, begun by inhaling, rocking back on front right heel, moving weight to back left foot, pulling right foot in as you turn 90 degrees to the left, then reaching over to grab your opponent, right hand under left.

(11) Continue by pulling opponent in as you drag left leg over next to right leg in a Semi-T Stance.

(12–13) And end by exhaling, stepping into a Left-Leg-Pointing (Slanted) Bow Stance, and shoving opponent away with a Press.

Do another Right Pull and Shove, stopping in a Right-Leg-Pointing (Slanted) Bow Stance (1 Breath).

Remember that each Pull and Shove move is done in one respiration and you concentrate on breathing as you rock back, reach, pull, and shove.

9. Toe Kick

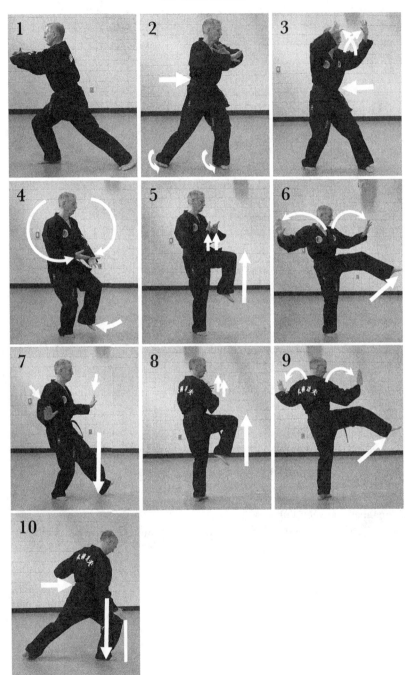

1 Right Pull and Shove (End)

(1) From last Right-Leg-Pointing (Slanted) Bow Stance of Right Pull and Shove (after 8/13)—

1 → 4 Left Twist Step (1 Breath)

(2–3) Inhale and begin Left Twist Step, pulling right foot in 90 degrees, turning around to the left (180–225 degrees, depending on how slanted to the right your last Right Pull and Shove was), and moving weight to left leg while twisting and bringing hands first sternum high in Cross Arms fashion then circling them above head (after which you begin to move weight back to right leg).

(4) Exhaling, complete turn to the left and move all weight back to right leg as you drag left leg close to the right leg in a Semi-T Stance, dropping hands down in front of your body, wrist to wrist, palms toward body, left (kicking side) hand outside (completing first part of Cross Arms).

4 → 6 Left-Foot Toe Kick (1 Breath)

(5) Then, without pause, inhale again, pulling left leg up into a Right-Leg-Supported Golden Rooster Stance, hands, continuing Cross Arms movement, also coming up, but stopping sternum high.

(6) From there, exhale as you extend left leg out into a toe kick, knee almost locked, toes extended outwards, arms/hands moving into Balance Position.

6 → 9 Right-Foot Toe Kick (1 Breath)

(7) Exhalation and kick completed, step forward by dropping left kicking leg down.

(8) Then, inhaling, bring right leg up into a Left-Leg-Supported Golden Rooster Stance, leg and arms in mirror Cross Arms position.

(9) Before exhaling and extending right leg out into a toe kick, arms/hands in opposite Balance Position.

9 → 10 Right-Leg-Pointing Bow Stance

(10) End by dropping right leg down into a Right-Leg-Pointing Bow Stance. Toe Kick is much like Heel Kick, except the kick is done with the tips of the toes and knee does not completely lock.

10. Moving Hammer Fist Block to Parry and Vertical Hammer Fist

1 Right-Leg-Pointing Bow Stance (End of Right-Foot Toe Kick)

(1) From a Right-Leg-Pointing Bow Stance after Right-Foot Toe Kick (**9/10**)—

1 → 3 Left Twist Step (½ Breath)

(2) Inhale and begin another Left Twist Step, rocking back, pulling right foot in 90 degrees, moving weight to back left leg, and starting 180-degree turn to left.

(3) Then, still inhaling, complete 180-degree turn to the left by pulling left leg in close and moving weight back to the right leg, at the same time dropping left fist down under open right hand, which is parallel to the plane of the floor.

3 → 4 Left-Fist Moving Hammer Block (½ Breath)

(4) Continuing, lift up left foot, then, beginning to exhale, drop it down on to its heel in a **Right-Leg-Supported Left-Heel Empty Stance**, at the same time bringing left fist up, around, and down again in a Left-Fist Moving Hammer Block, right hand dropping to the side, palm down and parallel to the plane of the floor.

Note that the stance of this Hammer Fist Block is different from that in **8/3–5** above.

4 → 6 Left Hook and Right Parry (½ Breath)

(5–6) Inhaling again, open fist and turn hand 270 degrees, first inward then outward, grab opponent's arm with Left-Hand Hook, and step forward with a Right-Leg Front Step while pulling opponent's arm with hook hand and parrying with right open hand.

6 → 7 Left Vertical Hammer Fist (½ Breath)

(7) Then, exhaling, complete Right-Leg Front Step by moving into a Right-Leg-Pointing Bow Stance as you strike opponent in solar plexus area with circling Left Vertical Hammer Fist, right hand open and stopping just inside the crook of the left arm.

7 → 9 Right-Fist Moving Hammer Block (1 Breath)

(8) From Right-Leg-Pointing Bow Stance (in Step **7**), inhale and move weight to back left leg as you pull front right leg back, at same time dropping right fist down under left hand, now open and parallel to the plane of the floor.

(9) Continuing, pick right leg up, then, beginning to exhale, drop it down in a **Left-Leg-Supported Right-Heel Empty Stance**, while bringing right fist up, around, and down in a Right-Fist Moving Hammer Block, left hand dropping to the side, palm down and parallel to the plane of the floor.

9 → 11 Right Hook and Left Parry (½ Breath)

(10–11) Without pause and inhaling again, grab opponent's arm with Right-Hand Hook, and step ahead with a Left-Leg Front Step, pulling opponent's arm with hook hand while parrying with left open hand.

11 → 12 Right Vertical Hammer Fist (½ Breath)

(12) Finally, exhaling, complete Left-Leg Front Step into Left-Leg-Pointing Bow Stance, striking opponent's solar plexus with circling Right Vertical Hammer Fist, left hand open and stopping just inside the crook of right arm.

Do one more Left-Fist Moving Hammer Block to Left Hook and Right Parry, followed by Left Vertical Hammer Fist, ending in a Right-Leg-Pointing Bow Stance (2 Breaths).

11. White Serpent Flicks its Tongue

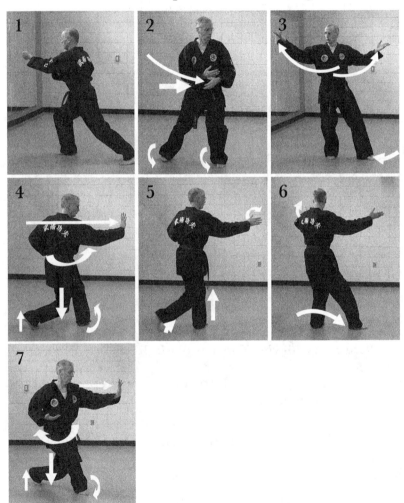

1 Right-Leg-Pointing Bow Stance (End of Left Vertical Hammer Fist)

(1) From a Right-Leg-Pointing Bow Stance of Left Vertical Hammer Fist (after 10/12)—

1 → 3 Left Twist Step with Right-Leg-Supported Empty Stance (½ Breath)

(2) Inhale, begin Left Twist Step, rocking back, pulling right foot in 90 degrees, and moving weight to back left leg as you begin to turn 180 degrees to your left.

(3) Continuing to inhale, complete 180-degree turn to the left, moving weight back to right leg, and pulling left leg in close into a Right-Leg-Supported Empty Stance, while also bringing arms up in Crescent Hands position.

3 → 4 Right-Hand White Serpent Flicks its Tongue (½ Breath)

(4) From Right-Leg-Supported Empty Stance with Crescent Hands, exhale as you bend knees and sink while turning hips to the left and squeezing thighs inwards slightly, at the same time striking opponent low with a Right-Hand Palm Thrust, left hand stopping on the left hip, palm up. This is called **Half Right-Hand White Serpent Flicks its Tongue.**

4 → 6 Left-Leg-Supported Empty Stance (½ Breath)

(5–6) Inhaling, stand up and take a Right-Leg Front Step into a Left-Leg-Supported Empty Stance, with an opposite Crescent Hands position.

6 → 7 Left-Hand White Serpent Flicks its Tongue (½ Breath)

(7) Then, exhaling, bend knees and sink while turning hips to the opposite or right direction and squeezing thighs inward slightly, at the same time striking opponent low with a Left-Hand Palm Thrust. This is called **Half Left-Hand White Serpent Flicks its Tongue.**

End with another Half Right-Hand White Serpent Flicks its Tongue move.

One can do a more difficult variation of this move, the **Complete White Serpent Flicks its Tongue**, by sitting on the back heel after completing the Palm Thrusts. Attempt this more difficult move only after sufficient practice, keeping back straight as you sit down and stand up, following striking hands with eyes.

12. Grasping Hook to Bow Stance and Golden Rooster

1 Right-Hand White Serpent Flicks its Tongue (End)

(1) After completing last Half Right-Hand White Serpent Flicks its Tongue (after 11/7)—

1 → 5 Right-Hand Grasping Hook (1 Breath)

(2–3) Inhale, bringing right leg forward and stepping ahead into a side-facing Left-Leg-Supported T Stance, simultaneously putting left hand on hip and moving right open hand, fingers pointing down and about thigh high, across the front in a sweeping **Right-Hand Push Block** move.

(4–5) Then, exhaling, move to the right into a Right-Leg-Supported T Stance, circling right hand up and out into a Right-Hand Grasping Hook, the Grasping Hook about shoulder height, at a 45-degree angle to the rear, elbow bent at about a 135-degree angle, and left hand, palm up, just about touching the funny bone in right arm.

In Steps 2–5, eyes are always following right hand.

5 → 7 Right-Leg-Supported Side Squat (1 Breath)

(6) Next, as you begin to inhale again, look to your left, bringing left leg half up.

(7) Then exhale, sliding left leg out into a Right-Leg-Supported Side Squat Stance.

7 → 8 Left-Leg-Pointing Bow Stance

(8) Which, as you continue exhaling, smoothly transitions into a Left-Leg-Pointing Bow Stance, left hand in front, palm facing out, index finger about nose high, right hand trailing behind, still in Grasping Hook.

8 → 11 Left-Leg-Supported Golden Rooster to Left-Hand Grasping Hook (1 Breath)

(9) From this Left-Leg-Pointing Bow Stance, begin to inhale again, bringing right leg up into a Left-Leg-Supported Golden Rooster Stance, right hand in front, left hand off to the side, palm parallel to the plane of the floor.

(10–11) Then, without hesitation, smoothly turn your body left 90 degrees and, exhaling, drop right leg down into a Left-Leg Supported T Stance while bringing left hand up into a mirror-image Left-Hand Grasping Hook, right hand coming up and over, palm now down, just about touching left elbow.

11 → 13 Left-Leg-Supported Side Squat Stance (1 Breath)

(12) From that Left-Leg-Supported T Stance, inhale as you bring right leg up.

(13) Then, exhaling, smoothly slide right leg into a Left-Leg-Supported Side Squat Stance.

13 → 14 Right-Leg-Pointing Bow Stance

(14) Which, as you continue exhaling, smoothly transitions into a Right-Leg-Pointing Bow Stance, right hand in front, palm open, left hand trailing behind, still in Grasping Hook.

Note the shape of left hand in trailing Grasping Hook (12/14).

14 → 18 Right-Leg Supported Golden Rooster to Separation Stance (2 Breaths)

(15) End by first inhaling and bringing left leg up into a Right-Leg-Supported Golden Rooster, left hand in front, right hand off to the side, palm parallel to the plane of the floor.

(16) Then, exhaling, drop left leg and left hand down as you begin turning body 90 degrees to the left into a Separation Stance.

(17–18) Whereupon, inhaling again, bring arms up in front, palms down, shoulder height, then, exhaling, drop arms to side.

Steps **15–18** can also be done in one breath (inhaling during Step **15**, at the end of which, right arm first rises as body turns 90 degrees to the left then drops together with left arm and left leg while exhaling in Steps **16–18**).

Closing

Reference 12 *Qigong* Breathing Techniques, Closing, if you still need more details on this ending.

4

Forms

Forms are a combination of what are called frames or "postures" practiced in a predetermined and set order. In very general terms, the English word "posture" usually refers to the stationary positioning of the body, a pose. Taiji does incorporate stances, which some might see as unmoving, but the emphasis is on movement in and between these stances, as well as the added non-stationary hand and/or leg techniques. The term "posture" as used here, therefore, might best be understood as a maneuver or move, the most common of which are the 12 Basic Moves introduced in Chapter 3. And Forms should be seen as a series of such moves which, when practiced correctly, comprise a continuous rhythmical progression from one move to the next, one ending only to be followed without pause by another, until a particular Form is completed, with the opening and closing of those moves paralleling or matching inhalations and exhalations.

The Forms introduced in this chapter include 8 Postures, 10 Postures, 16 Postures, and 24 Postures.[1] The number of postures counted in a Form that go into making up the name for that Form includes everything between, but not including, the beginning and ending Preparatory Stances. However, in some Forms the same posture is repeated and generally, though not always, those repeated postures are not counted separately, but as one. In 8 Postures, for example, #s 2–7 are all repeated, but only counted once each.

---

1   32 Postures, 42 Postures, and 48 Postures being other commonly practiced New Style Forms that make up the next or intermediate stage of Taiji.

Among these different Forms, 8 Postures is not commonly practiced. In fact, frequently 10 Postures is mistakenly called 8 Postures.[2] However, 8 Postures and 10 Postures as introduced here are quite different, with 8 Postures included because it is a relatively easy Form to learn for the beginner. The remaining three Forms, 10 Postures, 16 Postures, and 24 Postures, are the most popular Taiji Forms. They can be seen practiced in China and other countries in places as common as public parks or in more confined areas like Taiji studios—where the performance of 24 Postures is usually used to determine one's eligibility for advancement to the rank of black belt in *Taijiquan*.

As was the case with the Basic Stances, 12 *Qigong* Breathing Techniques, 3 Steps, and 12 Basic Moves, readers are encouraged to first watch the relevant videos for the individual Forms (video titles being identical to Form names) before reading these explanations. Done in that way, the explanations should then help them better understand exactly how to practice the Forms. In time and with regular practice, one will no longer need either the videos or the explanations.

8 POSTURES
1. Opening (2 Breaths)

(1) From Preparatory Stance—

(2–3) Move to Separation Stance.

Reference 12 *Qigong* Breathing Techniques, Opening, if still in need of more details on coordinating movement, transfer of weight, and breathing.

---

2   When the Opening and Closing in 10 Postures are not counted.

2. Tiger Opens its Mouth—Twice (2 Breaths)

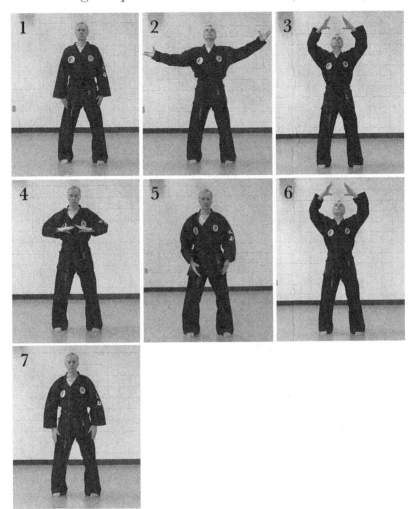

(1) In Separation Stance (1/3)—

(2–7) Slowly do Tiger Opens its Mouth twice, ending in Separation Stance.

Reference 12 *Qigong* Breathing Techniques, #1, Tiger Opens its Mouth, for more details on coordinating movement and breathing.

3. Bend Knees Palm Press—Twice (2 Breaths)

(1) Still in Separation Stance (2/7)—

(2–5) Do Bend Knees Palm Press twice, the second one ending with knees still bent, hands pushing down toward thighs.

Reference 12 *Qigong* Breathing Techniques, #2, Bend Knees Palm Press, for more details on coordinating movement and breathing.

4. Fist Beneath the Elbow—Twice (2 Breaths)

(1) From bent-knees position of Bend Knees Palm Press (3/5), hands pushing down toward thighs—

(2–3) Begin to inhale and rotate hips right 45 degrees, simultaneously picking up right leg and first dropping then bringing arms/hands out, around, and up.

(4) Next, without pause, exhale and drop right leg down into a Left-Leg-Supported (Slanted) Right-Heel Empty Stance, arms/hands moving into a Raised Hands Position, except for left hand, which is not open, but closed in a fist. This is a **Left Fist Beneath the Elbow.**

(5) Inhaling again, and moving weight to right leg, pick up left leg and turn hips left 45 degrees, while first dropping then bringing arms/hands out, around, and up.

(6) After which, exhaling, drop left leg down into a Right-Leg-Supported (Slanted) Left-Heel Empty Stance, arms/hands moving into a mirror Raised Hands Position, except for the right hand which is again a closed fist. This is a **Right Fist Beneath the Elbow.**

5. Roll Away Forearm (Repulse Monkey)—Four Times (4 Breaths)

(1) From Right Fist Beneath the Elbow (in Left-Heel Empty Stance [4/6])—

(2) Move to regular Empty Stance by touching ball of left foot to ground while inhaling and bringing hands up in a Crescent Arms position, following right hand with eyes as it rises up (at a 45-degree angle to the rear, arm bent at about a 135-degree angle, index finger about ear height).

(3–6) Continuing without pause, and as you begin to exhale, do Left-Leg Back Step and complete Right-Hand Repulse Monkey, followed by three more Repulse Monkeys in succession (Left, Right, Left).

Ending in a Right-Leg-Supported Empty Stance with Left-Hand Palm Thrust (Step 6).

Reference 12 Basic Moves, #2, Roll Away Forearm (Repulse Monkey), Steps 2–8, for a side view of the movements in a Right-Hand and a Left-Hand Repulse Monkey, along with more details on coordinating movement, transfer of weight, and breathing in them.

6. Part the Wild Horse's Mane—Twice (2 Breaths)

(1) From Right-Leg-Supported Empty Stance in Left-Hand Repulse Monkey (5/6)—

(2) Begin inhaling, drag the left leg toward the right leg into a Semi-T Stance and Grab the Ball, left hand under right.

(3) Then, turning left 45 degrees, exhale and step into a Left-Hand (Slanted) Part the Wild Horse's Mane.

(4–5) Follow this by turning right 90 degrees and stepping into a mirror-image Right-Hand (Slanted) Part the Wild Horse's Mane, breathing appropriately.

Reference 12 Basic Moves, #1, Part the Wild Horse's Mane, Steps 4–8, for more details on coordinating movement, transfer of weight, and breathing.

7. Grasping Hook to Single Whip—Twice (2 Breaths)

(1) From Right-Leg Pointing Bow Stance of Right-Hand (Slanted) Part the Wild Horse's Mane (6/5)—

(2) Inhale, dragging left leg up next to the right leg in a Semi-T Stance, simultaneously forming right hand into a Right-Hand Grasping Hook, left hand palm up and just about touching the right elbow.

(3) Then, exhaling, with left leg step out left 90 degrees into a (Slanted) Bow Stance, left hand with open palm extended out directly in front, elbow slightly bent, left index finger at nose height, and back Right-Hand Grasping Hook maintaining same position.

This is called a **Left-Hand (Slanted) Single Whip**.

(4) Without pause, and inhaling again, drag the right leg up to the left leg into another Semi-T Stance, hands simultaneously forming a mirror-image Left-Hand Grasping Hook.

(5) Then, exhaling, with right leg step out right 90 degrees into a mirror-image **Right-Hand (Slanted) Single Whip**.

8. Return and Closing (2 or 3 Breaths)

(1) From Right-Leg-Pointing Bow Stance in Right-Hand (Slanted) Single Whip (7/5)—

(2) Begin to inhale, moving weight to back left leg, letting arms/hands drop into first part of Cross Arms, right hand inside left, and pulling right foot inward 45 degrees.

(3) Then exhale as you move weight back to right leg, pulling left leg over to right leg into a knees-still-bent Separation Stance, arms/hands now pulled up and crossed, palms facing inward, left hand inside right.

(4) Without pause, inhale again as you rise, bringing arms/hands out in front, palms down, until you stand almost erect, arms extending straight out front about shoulder height.

(5) At which time you exhale and drop arms to your side.

Steps 1–5 are called **Left-Leg Return**.

Note that Steps 2–5 can be done in two complete respirations, although doing them in one is also possible.

(6) Still in Separation Stance (Step 5), do Closing, paying attention to correct breathing.

10 POSTURES
1. Opening (2 Breaths) to Bend Knees Palm Press (1 Breath)

(1) From Preparatory Stance—

(2) Move to Separation Stance.

(3–4) In Separation Stance do one Bend Knees Palm Press, ending with knees still bent, hands pushing down toward thighs.

2. High Pat on Horse—Twice (2 Breaths)

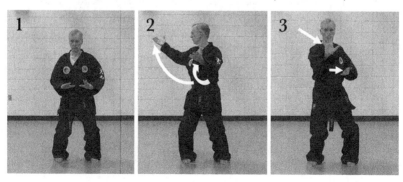

(1) From bent-knees position of Bend Knees Palm Press (1/4), hands pushing down toward thighs—

(2) Begin to inhale, bringing hands up into a Crescent Hands position, left hand in front, right hand off to the rear and side.

(3) Then, without pause and watching the right hand, exhale and do a Right-Hand Palm Thrust directly to front, exhalation ending as Palm Thrust is completed and left hand, palm up, reaches just above hip.

(4) Next, again without pause, begin to inhale and do a mirror-image Crescent Hands, turning right front hand palm up, moving left hand up and off to the rear and side.

(5) Then exhale and do a mirror-image Left-Hand Palm Thrust.

Although Steps 2–3 and 4–5 are usually called **Right-Hand High Pat on Horse** and **Left-Hand High Pat on Horse**, respectively, some also refer to them as Right-Hand and Left-Hand Repulse Monkey.

3. Brush Knee—Twice (2 Breaths)

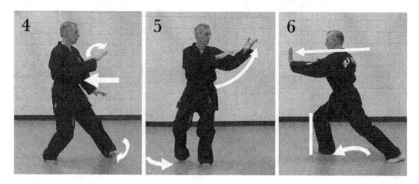

(1) Still in the bent-knees position, at the end of Left-Hand High Pat on Horse (2/5)—

(2–3) Begin to inhale and, pulling left foot up next to right foot in a Semi-T Stance, turn left 90 degrees, first moving into a Left-Right-Hands Brush Knee Strike Ready Position, then exhaling and stepping into and completing a Left-Right-Hands Brush Knee.

(4) Next, inhaling again, and beginning to turn right 180 degrees, do a Right Twist Step by first rocking back on front left heel, turning left foot inward 90 degrees, and moving weight from front left foot to back right foot.

(5) After which, still inhaling, and continuing to turn body right, move weight back to left foot as you drag right foot back into a Right-Left-Hands Brush Knee Strike Ready Position.

(6) Then, exhaling, step into and complete a Right-Left-Hands Brush Knee.

Compare Right Twist Step in Steps **4–5** here with Right Twist Step in Basic Steps, Carry the Water Barrel, Steps **7–8**.

4. Part the Wild Horse's Mane—Twice (2 Breaths)

(1) From completed Right-Left-Hands Brush Knee (3/6)—

(2–3) As you inhale, begin turning left 180 degrees doing a Left Twist Step by rocking back on front right heel, turning right foot inward 90 degrees, and moving weight from front right foot to back left foot. After which, still inhaling, and continuing to turn body left, move weight back to right foot as you drag the left foot back into a Semi-T Stance and Grab the Ball.

(4) Then step out into a Left-Hand Part the Wild Horse's Mane.

(5–7) Reversing course, turn right 180 degrees doing a Right Twist Step, Grab the Ball, and then step out into a mirror-image Right-Hand Part the Wild Horse's Mane.

Concentrate on rocking back and forth, moving weight from one leg to the other, in rhythm with your breathing.

Reference 12 Basic Moves, #7, Overhead Block and Palm Thrust, Steps 2–3 for comparison with Left Twist Step here. For help coordinating movement, transfer of weight, and breathing with Right Twist, reference 10 Postures, #3, Brush Knee, Steps 4–5 just above.

5. Cloud Hands—Three Times (3 Breaths)

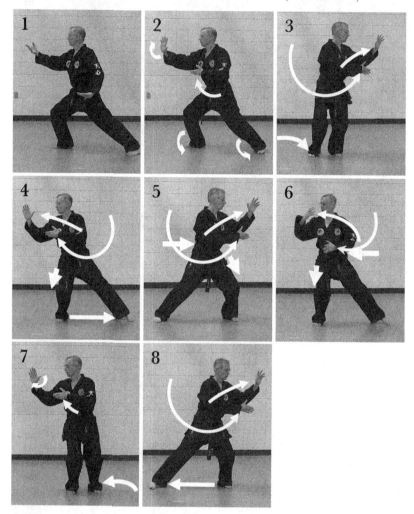

(1) From Right-Hand Part the Wild Horse's Mane (4/7)—

(2) Inhale as you begin to rotate feet left and bring hands up into a Right-Facing Cloud Hands Defensive Position (with small or medium Right-Leg-Supported Side Squat Stance).

(3) Then, as you begin to exhale, move weight to left leg, dragging right leg and completing Left-Leg Side Step, stopping in Separation Stance with hand placement of Left-Facing Cloud Hands Defensive Position.

(4) Inhaling, move left leg out, forming another Right-Facing Cloud Hands Defensive Position (with small or medium Right-Leg-Supported Side Squat Stance).

(5) Then begin to repeat Step 3 by exhaling and moving weight to left leg but stopping in a Left-Facing Cloud Hands Defensive Position (and not dragging right leg into a Separation Stance).

(6–7) From Left-Facing Cloud Hands Defensive Position, turn right 180 degrees and, inhaling, first move weight to right leg as you begin rotating hands in same direction, then drag left leg into a Separation Stance, with hand placement stopping in Right-Facing Cloud Hands Defensive Position.

(8) Next, exhaling, slide right leg out, forming a Left-Facing Cloud Hands Defensive Position (again a small or medium Left-Leg Supported Side Squat Stance)—not a Separation Stance.

Breathing in Steps 6–8 effectively reverses the pattern described in Basic Steps, #3, Side Step and 12 Basic Moves, #5, Cloud Hands; as well as Steps 2–4 just above.

Note difference between Left- or Right-Facing Cloud Hands Defensive Position and Separation Stance with hand placement of Left- or Right-Facing Cloud Hands Defensive Position.

6. Reach and Pull (1 Breath)

(1) From Left-Facing Cloud Hands Defensive Position (5/8)—

(2–3) Move weight to right leg and do Right Reach and Pull, inhaling as you reach up to your right, then exhaling as you pull down, stopping when arms/ hands just reach midpoint of body and weight begins to transfer back to left leg.

Reference 12 *Qigong* Breathing Techniques, #7, Reach and Pull, for help remembering movement of body weight and breathing.

7. Golden Rooster—Twice (2 Breaths)

(1) Having completed Right Reach and Pull **(6/3)**—

(2) Inhale again as you bring right leg up and move directly into a Left-Leg-Supported Golden Rooster Stance.

(3–4) Then exhale, dropping right leg, after which, inhaling again, pick up left leg forming a mirror-image Right-Leg-Supported Golden Rooster Stance.

8. Heel Kick—Twice (2 Breaths)

(1) From Right-Leg Supported Golden Rooster Stance (7/4)—

(2) Still inhaling slightly, circle arms/hands above head.

(3–4) After which, exhaling, step out and down on to left leg and begin Cross Arms, dropping arms/hands down, palms facing inward, wrist to wrist, just above stomach, before inhaling again and bringing right leg and arms/hands up to about waist to sternum height, kicking hand on the outside.

(5) From where, exhaling, you do a Right-Foot Heel Kick 45 degrees to the right.

(6–7) Next, drop right leg and step into a Right-Leg Supported Golden Rooster Stance followed by a Left-Foot Heel Kick 45 degrees to the left, breathing appropriately.

Pay attention to Balance Position of arms in Heel Kicks, referencing 12 Basic Moves, #4, Heel Kick, Steps 6 and 9 if necessary.

9. Grasp the Swallow's Tail—Twice (6 Breaths)

(1) From Right-Leg-Supported Golden Rooster Stance after completing Left-Foot Heel Kick (8/7)—

(2) Drop left foot straight down, turn right 90 degrees, and, while inhaling, pull right leg up next to left leg in a Semi-T Stance and Grab the Ball.

(3–8) Then step into a Right-Leg-Supported Bow Stance and complete a Right Grasp the Swallow's Tail, breathing appropriately.

(9–10) Right Grasp the Swallow's Tail completed, begin to turn left 180 degrees doing a Left Twist Step.

(11–16) Immediately followed by movement into a mirror-image Left Grasp the Swallow's Tail—starting with Left-Arm Ward Off and ending in Left-Leg-Supported Bow Stance, hands in completed Bow Stance Push position.

Reference 12 Basic Moves, #6, Grasp the Swallow's Tail, Steps 3–13, for more details on coordinating movement, transfer of weight, and breathing. To help remember Left Twist Step, reference 12 Basic Moves, #7, Overhead Block and Palm Thrust, Steps 2–3, and 10 Postures, #4, Part the Wild Horse's Mane, Steps 2–3.

10. Return and Closing (3 Breaths)

(1) From Left-Leg-Supported Bow Stance after finishing Left Grasp the Swallow's Tail, hands still in completed Bow Stance Push (9/16)—

(2) Inhale and, as you begin to move weight to the back right foot, pull left foot in 90 degrees, hips turning right as you do so, right foot beginning to move outward, arms following hips.

(3) Then, without pause, exhale and turn right foot out 90 degrees as you bring right arm/hand up, out, and over the right leg in what has become a Right-Leg-Supported Side Squat Stance.

(4) From Right-Leg-Supported Side Squat Stance, inhaling, begin moving weight to back left leg and, as you drop arms/hands down in front of you, palms

facing inward, wrist to wrist, left hand inside right hand, both just in front of the belly button, drag right leg over into a Separation Stance.

(5) From which, continuing to inhale, stand, bringing arms/hands up in a half Cross Arms move until they are extended out in front of you, palms down.

(6) Finally, exhale as you let arms/hands fall down and to your side.

Steps **2–6** are called **Right-Leg Return**.

(7) Still in Separation Stance, do Closing, again paying attention to correct breathing.

16 POSTURES
1. Opening (2 Breaths)

(1) From Preparatory Stance—

(2) Move to Separation Stance.

2. Bend Knees Palm Press (1 Breath)

(1) Still in Separation Stance (1/2)—

(2) Do Bend Knees Palm Press, ending with knees still bent, hands pushing down toward thighs.

3. Part the Wild Horse's Mane—Twice (2 Breaths)

(1) From bent-knees position of Bend Knees Palm Press (2/3), hands pushing toward thighs—

(2–3) Turn left 90 degrees, Grab the Ball, and step into a Left-Hand Part the Wild Horse's Mane.

(4) Heading in same direction, follow this up with a Right-Hand Part the Wild Horse's Mane.

Pay attention to rocking-back-and-forth movement and corresponding breathing. If necessary, reference 3 Basic Steps, #1, Front Step, and 12 Basic Moves, #1, Part the Wild Horse's Mane.

4. White Crane Displays its Wings (1 Breath)

(1) From Right-Leg-Pointing Bow Stance of Right-Hand Part the Wild Horse's Mane (3/4)—

(2) Inhale, bringing back left foot up behind front right foot as you move left hand forward in a knee-high Left-Hand Push Block to the right, right open hand moving over and touching just inside the crook of the left arm.

(3) Then, continuing to inhale, turn hips left as you bring left arm, right hand still nestled in its crook, over and up until left hand is directly across from left ear, palm facing inward.

(4) Next, exhaling, move front right leg ahead, stepping into a Left-Leg Supported Empty Stance, at the same time turning hips right, back to original front-facing position, while moving right hand down to the right side of your body, just below the hip, palm parallel to the plane of the floor.

Steps **2–4** are called **Left-Leg-Supported White Crane Displays its Wings**.

5. Double Cross Block to Brush Knee and Brush Knee (2 Breaths)

(1) From Left-Leg-Supported White Crane Displays its Wings (4/4)—

(2) Inhaling, turn hips to the right, using left forearm in a **Cross-Body Left-Forearm Block** to the right.

(3–4) Then, still inhaling, as you rotate hips back to the left, pull front right leg back close to left leg in a Semi-T Stance, at the same time dropping left arm first down, then up, while using right hand, palm open, in a sternum-high **Right-Hand Cross Block** to the left that becomes part of a Right-Left-Hands Brush Knee Strike Ready Position.

(5) Next, and without pause, exhale and step ahead into a Right-Left-Hands Brush Knee.

(6) Follow this with a Left-Right-Hands Brush Knee.

6. Moving Hammer Fist Block to Parry and Vertical Hammer Fist (2 Breaths)

(1) From Left-Leg-Pointing Bow Stance of Left-Right-Hands Brush Knee (5/6)—

(2–3) Inhaling, rock back then begin a Right-Leg Front Step, while dropping right fist down under left hand, which is parallel to the plane of the floor.

(4) But instead of stepping out into a Right-Leg-Supported Bow Stance, exhaling, drop right leg down directly in front into a Left-Leg-Supported Right-Heel Empty Stance as you bring right fist up inside left arm, around, and then down in a Right-Fist Moving Hammer Block, left hand stopping at side, palm down and parallel to the plane of the floor.

(5) Next move ahead with Right Hook and Left Parry.

(6) Followed by a Right Vertical Hammer Fist.

Note that the movement in Steps 2–3 here to Right-Heel Empty Stance is forward, not backward, thus different from 12 Basic Moves, #10, Moving Hammer Fist Block to Parry and Vertical Hammer Fist, Steps 2–6.

7. Bow Stance Push (1 Breath)

(1) From Left-Leg-Pointing Bow Stance of Right Vertical Hammer Fist (6/6)—

(2–3) Rock back and do two-handed Bow Stance Push, paying attention to coordinating rocking-back-and-forth movement, transfer of weight, and breathing.

8. Grasping Hook to Single Whip (1 Breath)

(1) Still in Left-Leg-Pointing Bow Stance, arms/hands now extended straight out in front after Bow Stance Push (7/3)—

(2) Inhaling, pull left leg in close to right leg in a Semi-T Stance, turning hips right 90 degrees, all while moving arms/hands back and to the right 135 degrees into a Right-Hand Grasping Hook.

(3) Then, from Right-Hand Grasping Hook, exhaling, turn hips left 90 degrees and step back to the front into a Left-Hand Single Whip.

9. Play the Lute (1 Breath)

(1) In Left-Leg-Pointing Bow Stance of Left-Hand Single Whip (8/3)—

(2) Inhale and bring back right foot up behind front left foot as you turn your hips slightly to the left and move right hand across the front of your body, in a slow Right-Hand Cross Block.

(3–4) Then, still inhaling, pick up front left foot, and as you exhale drop it down into a Right-Leg-Supported Left-Heel Empty Stance, and rotate hips back to the right, all while bringing arms/hands up and then down into a Raised Hands Position.

Hands move in an undulating manner, following the turning of the hips, and as if strumming a stringed musical instrument.

10. Roll Away Forearm (Repulse Monkey)—Twice (2 Breaths)

(1) From Right-Leg-Supported Left-Heel Empty Stance of Play the Lute (9/4)—

(2) Move to regular Empty Stance by touching ball of left foot to ground, then, inhaling, bringing arms/hands up in a Crescent Arms position.

(3) Continuing without pause, exhale, doing Left-Leg Back Step and completing Right-Hand Repulse Monkey.

(4) Followed by a Left-Hand Repulse Monkey.

For more details on coordinating movement, transfer of weight, and breathing, reference the 12 Basic Moves, #2, Roll Away Forearm (Repulse Monkey), and 8 Postures, #5, Roll Away Forearm (Repulse Monkey).

11. Slanted Twist Step to Double Overhead Block and Palm Thrust (2 Breaths)

(1) From Right-Leg-Supported Empty Stance of Left-Hand Repulse Monkey (10/4)—

(2) Inhaling, pull left foot in 90 degrees, then move weight from back right leg to front left leg, all while beginning to turn hips to the right about 135 degrees. This is a **Slanted Right Twist Step**.

(3) Still inhaling, continue, and as you move to Grab the Ball, left hand under right, pick up right leg.

(4–5) Then, exhaling, turn right foot to the right and step out, dropping it on the ground, after which, stepping out 45 degrees to the left with a Left-Leg Front Step, carry out a (Slanted) Left-Hand Palm Block with a Right-Hand Palm Thrust.

(6) Follow this by turning right 90 degrees, moving weight to right leg, and undulating arms in a wave-like movement.

(7) After which, move weight back to left leg, pull right foot in close in a Semi-T Stance, and Grab the Ball.

(8) Then step out into a (Slanted) Right-Hand Overhead Block with a Left-Hand Palm Thrust.

Compare with similar movements in 12 Basic Moves, #7, Overhead Block and Palm Thrust.

12. Needle at the Bottom of the Ocean (1 Breath)

(1) From Right-Leg Pointing Bow Stance of (Slanted) Right-Hand Overhead Block with Left-Hand Palm Thrust (11/8)—

(2) Inhaling, and turning hips 45 degrees to the left, pull left foot up behind front right foot as right hand moves across front of body, sternum high, in a

Right-Hand Cross Block to the left, left hand, palm open, first dropping down, then sliding up along the left side of the body.

(3–4) Next, beginning to exhale, move right leg out in front into a Left-Leg Supported Empty Stance as right hand, having finished Cross Block, now circles back, down and to the right of the body, where it stops, just below the hip, palm parallel to the plane of the floor, while left hand, having reached left shoulder, moves down directly in front of the body, fingers reaching down into an imaginary ocean.

Steps **2–4** complete a **Left-Hand Needle at the Bottom of the Ocean**, all in one breath.

13. Fan Through Back (1 Breath)

(1) From Left-Leg-Supported Empty Stance of Left-Hand Needle at the Bottom of the Ocean (**12/4**)—

(2) Inhaling, stand up, at the same time bringing left and right open hands toward body, sternum high, right-hand palm up against inside of left wrist.

(3) Then, beginning to exhale, step out into a Right-Leg-Pointing Bow Stance, right hand extending straight out about sternum height in a Palm Thrust, left hand moving off to the left, left elbow bent at about a 125-degree angle, left arm almost parallel with the plane of floor, palm open outward at about ear height.

The movements in Steps **2–3** complete what is often called a **Right-Hand Fan Through Back**.

14. Push Block to Double Cloud Hands (2 Breaths)

(1) From Right-Leg-Pointing Bow Stance of Right-Hand Fan Through Back (13/3)—

(2) Inhaling and rotating feet to left, transfer weight to back left foot and move into a Left-Leg-Supported Side Squat Stance, at the same time using both open hands to push someone away toward the back left, left hand on top, right hand just below it. This is called a **Left-Right-Hands Double Push Block** and in this move functions as the first step in the Right-Leg Side Step in a Right-Moving Cloud Hands.

(3) Then, beginning to exhale, drag back left leg into a Separation Stance with a Right-Facing Cloud Hands Defensive Position.

(4–5) Follow this with another Right-Moving Cloud Hands that also ends in a Separation Stance with a Right-Facing Cloud Hands Defensive Position.

For help with such moves, reference the movement explanations in 12 Basic Moves, #5, Cloud Hands, and 10 Postures, #5, Cloud Hands.

15. Grasp the Swallow's Tail—Twice (6 Breaths)

(1) From the Separation Stance of Right-Facing Cloud Hands Defensive Position (14/5)—

(2–8) Inhaling, Grab the Ball and do a Right Grasp the Swallow's Tail.

(9–10) Finished, do a 180-degree Left Twist Step turn.

(11–16) Followed by a Left Grasp the Swallow's Tail.

For help with these movements, shifting of weight, and breathing, reference 12 Basic Moves, #6, Grasp the Swallow's Tail, Steps 3–13, and 10 Postures, #9, Grasp the Swallow's Tail, starting at Step 2.

16. Return and Closing (3 Breaths)

(1) From the Left-Leg-Supported Bow Stance Push found at the end of Left Grasp the Swallow's Tail, hands still in pushing position (15/16)—

(2–6) Do a Right-Leg Return.

(7) From Separation Stance at end of Right-Leg Return, do Closing.

Reference 10 Postures, #10, Return and Closing, for help with movements, shifting of weight, and breathing.

24 POSTURES
1. Opening (2 Breaths) to Bend
Knees Palm Press (1 Breaths)

(1) From Preparatory Stance—

(2) Move to Separation Stance.

(3–4) In Separation Stance do one Bend Knees Palm Press, ending with knees still bent, hands pushing down toward thighs.

2. Part the Wild Horse's Mane—
Three Times (3 Breaths)

(1) From bent-knees position of Bend Knees Palm Press, hands almost touching thighs (1/4)—

(2–3) Turn left 90 degrees and step into a Left-Hand Part the Wild Horse's Mane.

(4) Followed, moving in same direction, by a Right-Hand Part the Wild Horse's Mane.

(5) Then another Left-Hand Part the Wild Horse's Mane.

If still in need of more details on coordinating movement, transfer of weight, and breathing, again reference 12 Basic Moves, #1, Part the Wild Horse's Mane.

3. White Crane Displays its Wings (1 Breath)

(1) From the Left-Leg-Pointing Bow Stance of the second Left-Hand Part the Wild Horse's Mane (2/5)—

(2) Inhale, bringing back right foot up behind front left foot as you move right hand forward in a knee-high Right-Hand Push Block to the left, left open hand moving over and touching just inside the crook of the right arm.

(3) Then, continuing to inhale, turn hips right as you bring right arm, left hand still nestled in its crook, over and up until right hand is directly across from right ear, palm facing inward.

(4) Next, exhaling, move front left leg ahead, stepping into a Right-Leg Supported Empty Stance, at the same time turning hips left, back to original front-facing position, while moving left hand down to the left side of your body, just below the hip, palm parallel to the plane of the floor.

Steps **2–4** are called **Right-Leg-Supported White Crane Displays its Wings**, a mirror image of 16 Postures, #4, Left-Leg-Supported White Crane Displays its Wings, Steps **2–4**.

4. Double Cross Block to Triple
Brush Knee—(3 Breaths)

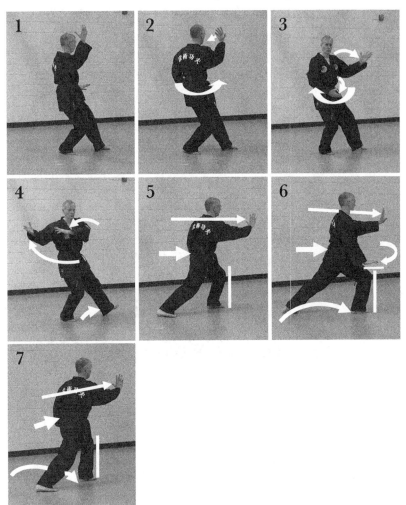

(1) From completed Right-Leg-Supported White Crane Displays its Wings (3/4)—

(2) Inhaling, turn hips to the left, using right forearm in a **Cross-Body Right-Forearm Block** to the left.

(3–4) Then, still inhaling, as you rotate hips back to the right, pull front left leg back close to right leg in a Semi-T Stance, at the same time using left hand, palm open, in a sternum-high **Left-Hand Cross Block** to the right that becomes part of a Left-Right-Hands Brush Knee Strike Ready Position.

(5) Next, without pause and exhaling, step ahead into a Left-Right-Hands Brush Knee.

(6) Followed, moving straight ahead, by a Right-Left-Hands Brush Knee.

(7) Then another Left-Right-Hands Brush Knee.

Steps **2–6** are a mirror image of Steps **2–6** in 16 Postures, #5, Double Cross Block to Brush Knee (with another Left-Right-Hands Brush Knee added here). For more details on coordinating movement, transfer of weight, and breathing, reference those steps in 16 Postures, #5, along with, if needed, 12 Basic Moves, #3, Brush Knee—again paying special attention to breathing, rocking back and forth, and movement of body weight from one leg to the other.

5. Play the Lute (1 Breath)

(1) From Left-Leg-Pointing Bow Stance of Left-Right-Hands Brush Knee (4/7)—

(2–3) Play the Lute. Start by inhaling and bringing back right foot up behind front left foot, turning hips slightly to the left and moving right hand across the front of your body in a slow Right-Hand Cross Block. After which, pick up front left foot and, as you exhale, drop it down into a Right-Leg-Supported Left-Heel Empty Stance, rotating hips back to the right, all while bringing arms/hands up then down into a Raised Hands Position.

For more details on coordinating movement, transfer of weight, and breathing, reference 16 Postures, #9, Play the Lute, Steps **1–4**.

6. Roll Away Forearm (Repulse Monkey)—Four Times (4 Breaths)

(1) From Left-Heel Empty Stance of Play the Lute (5/3)—

(2–3) Moving back, do a Right-Hand Repulse Monkey.

(4) Followed by a Left-Hand Repulse Monkey.

(5) Another Right-Hand Repulse Monkey.

(6) And one final Left-Hand Repulse Monkey.

Steps 1–4 are exactly the same as in 16 Postures, #10, Roll Away Forearm, Steps 1–4, with another Right-Hand and another Left-Hand Repulse Monkey added here, for a total of four such moves, not two. Reference 16 Postures, #10, then, for more details on coordinating movement, transfer of weight, and breathing.

7. Grasp the Swallow's Tail—Left (3 Breaths)

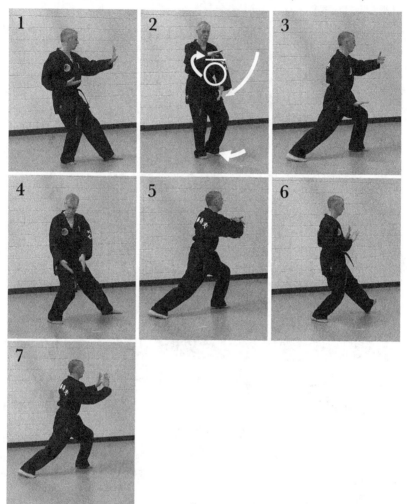

(1) From Right-Leg-Supported Empty Stance of Left-Hand Repulse Monkey (6/6)—

(2–7) Inhaling, pull left leg in close in Semi-T Stance, Grab the Ball, left hand under right, then exhale and step out into a Left-Arm Ward Off, followed by the remainder of a Left Grasp the Swallow's Tail (ending in Bow Stance Push).

Reference 10 Postures, #9, Grasp the Swallow's Tail, Steps **10–16**, for more details on coordinating the movement, transfer of weight, and breathing in Steps **3–7**.

8. Grasp the Swallow's Tail—Right (3 Breaths)

(1) From Left-Leg-Pointing Bow Stance Push at end of Left Grasp the Swallow's Tail (7/7)—

(2–3) Inhaling, turn 180 degrees doing a Right Twist Step, and again Grab the Ball, right hand under left.

(4–9) Then exhale and step out into a Right-Arm Ward Off, followed by the remainder of a Right Grasp the Swallow's Tail—all of which is a mirror image of the moves in #7, Left Grasp the Swallow's Tail, Steps 3–7, just above.

For more details on coordinating movement, transfer of weight, and breathing in Right Twist, reference 3 Basic Steps, Carry the Water Barrel, Steps 7–8, and

10 Postures, #3, Brush Knee, Steps **4–5**, along with #4, Part the Wild Horse's Mane, Steps **5–6**.

Reference 10 Postures, #9, Grasp the Swallow's Tail, Steps **2–8**, for details on coordinating movement, transfer of weight, and breathing in Steps **3–9**.

9. Double Push Block to Hook and Single Whip (1 Breath)

(1) From Right-Leg-Pointing Bow Stance of completed Right Grasp the Swallow's Tail (**8/9**), still in Bow Stance Push—

(2) Inhaling, turn hips to the left 90 degrees, transferring weight to back left foot and moving into a Left-Leg-Supported Side Squat Stance, at the same time doing a Left-Right-Hands Double Push Block to the left.

(3) From there, still inhaling and without pause, move weight back to right leg while pulling left leg in close to right leg in a Semi-T Stance and moving arms/hands back and to the right 135 degrees into a Right-Hand Hook.

(4) Then, from Right-Hand Hook, exhaling, turn hips left 90 degrees and step into a Left-Hand Single Whip.

10. Cloud Hands—Three Times (3 Breaths)

(1) From Left-Leg-Pointing Bow Stance of completed Left-Hand Single Whip (9/4)—

(2) Inhaling, turn feet and hips to the right 90 degrees, transferring weight to back right foot and moving into a Right-Leg-Supported Side Squat Stance, at the same time doing a Right-Facing Cloud Hands Defensive Position.

(3) From there, exhaling, drag right leg up into a Separation Stance with a Left-Facing Cloud Hands Defensive Position.

Combined, Steps 2–3 form a Left-Moving Cloud Hands.

(4–7) Follow this with two more Left-Moving Cloud Hands, the final one ending in a Separation Stance with a Left-Facing Cloud Hands Defensive Position.

Movements, transfer of weight, and breathing are all patterned on 12 Basic Moves, #5, Cloud Hands, Steps 2–6, which demonstrate two Cloud Hands left (with a third added here).

11. Grasping Hook to Single Whip (1 Breath)

(1) From Separation Stance with a Left-Facing Cloud Hands Defensive Position after the third and last Left-Moving Cloud Hands (10/7)—

(2) Inhaling, move arms/hands back and to the right 135 degrees into a Right-Hand Grasping Hook.

(3) Then, from Right-Hand Grasping Hook, exhaling, turn hips left 90 degrees and step into a Left-Hand Single Whip.

12. High Pat on Horse (1 Breath)

(1) From Left-Leg-Pointing Bow Stance of Left-Hand Single Whip (11/3)—

(2) Inhaling, bring back right foot up behind front left foot, at the same time moving hands into a Crescent Hands position, left hand in front, right hand off to the rear and side.

(3) Then, without pause and while stepping out with front left foot into a Right-Leg-Supported Empty Stance, exhale, completing a Right-Hand High Pat on Horse Palm Thrust.

13. Cross Arms to Heel Kick (2 Breaths)

(1) From Right-Leg-Supported Empty Stance of Right-Hand High Pat on Horse (12/3)—

(2-3) Pick up front left foot and, inhaling, cross arms/hands and move them above your head, then, without pause, exhale and move 45 degrees to the left, stepping out on to left leg as you begin dropping arms around and down in circular motion, after which, inhaling again, pull right leg up into a Left-Leg-Supported Golden Rooster Stance as you begin Cross Arms by bringing arms/hands up to just below the sternum, palms facing inward, wrist to wrist, right or kicking hand on the outside.

(4) From Left-Leg-Supported Golden Rooster Stance, exhaling, do Right-Foot Heel Kick 45 degrees to the right.

14. Double Knuckles Strike the Ears (1 Breath)

(1) From Left-Leg-Supported Golden Rooster Stance of Right-Foot Heel Kick (13/4)—

(2) Begin to inhale, bringing arms/hands down in close to sternum, fists closed, wrist to wrist, left arm inside right.

(3) Then, exhaling, step out right into Right-Leg-Pointing (Slanted) Bow Stance, fists first dropping down then going out in a large circular motion, around, up, and in, stopping with knuckles at ears (or temple areas) of an imaginary opponent.

Steps 2–3 are called **Right-Leg-Pointing Double Knuckles Strike the Ears.**

15. Heel Kick (1 Breath)

(1) From Right-Leg-Pointing (Slanted) Bow Stance of Double Knuckles Strike the Ears (**14/3**)—

(2) Inhaling, do Left Twist Step by beginning a 135-degree turn left, moving weight to back left leg as you circle arms/hands above your head.

(**3–4**) Then, still inhaling, as you move weight back to right leg, completing the 135-degree turn, begin Cross Arms, bringing arms/hands down, then up and in close, just below the sternum, palms facing inward, wrist to wrist, left or kicking hand on the outside, simultaneously pulling left leg in close and up into a Right-Leg-Supported Golden Rooster Stance.

(**5**) From which, without a pause and exhaling, do Left-Foot Heel Kick.

Reference Basic Moves, #4, Heel Kick, Steps **2–6**, for more details on co-ordinating movement, transfer of weight, and breathing.

16. Grasping Hook to Side Squat and Golden Rooster—Left (1½ Breaths)

(1) From Right-Leg-Supported Golden Rooster Stance of Left-Foot Heel Kick (15/5)—

(2) Drop left leg down close to right leg in a Right-Leg-Supported T Stance while moving hands to the right into a Right-Hand Grasping Hook, left hand, palm up, almost touching right elbow.

(3) Then, inhaling, look left, picking up left leg.

(4–5) After which, without pause and exhaling, slide the left leg left out to the left into a Right-Leg-Supported Side Squat Stance which easily transitions into a Left-Leg-Pointing Bow Stance, left hand, arm extended with elbow slightly bent, directly in front, palm open, and right hand dragging behind, still in Grasping Hook.

(6) Finally, inhaling, bring right leg up into a Left-Leg-Supported Golden Rooster Stance, complete with correct arm/hand positioning.

Except for Steps 1–2, movements, transfer of weight, and breathing all pattern 12 Basic Moves, #12, Grasping Hook to Bow Stance and Golden Rooster, Steps 5–9.

17. Grasping Hook to Side Squat and Golden Rooster—Right (1½ Breaths)

(1) From Left-Leg-Supported Golden Rooster Stance (16/6)—

(2) Turn hips left 90 degrees and begin exhaling, bringing right hand over the top and down near left arm, which has moved up forming a Left-Hand Grasping Hook, right hand, palm down, almost touching left elbow, right leg dropping down next to left leg in a Left-Leg-Supported T Stance.

(3) Then, inhaling, look right, picking up right leg.

(4–5) After which, without pause and exhaling, slide the right leg out to the right into a Left-Leg-Supported Side Squat Stance which easily transitions into a Right-Leg-Pointing Bow Stance, right hand, arm extended with elbow slightly bent, directly in front, palm open, and left hand dragging behind, still in Grasping Hook.

(6) Finally, inhaling again, bring left leg up into a Right-Leg-Supported Golden Rooster, complete with correct arm/hand positioning.

Reference Basic Moves, #12, Grasping Hook to Bow Stance and Golden Rooster, Steps 9–15, for more details on coordinating movement, transfer of weight, and breathing.

18. Overhead Block and Palm
Thrust—Twice (1½ Breaths)

(1) Continuing from Right-Leg-Supported Golden Rooster Stance (17/6)—

(2) Complete inhalation started in **17/6** as you move 45 degrees to the left, dropping your left foot down and Grabbing the Ball, right hand under left.

(3) Then turn hips right 90 degrees and, exhaling, step out into (Slanted) Right-Hand Palm Block with a Left-Hand Palm Thrust.

(4–5) Follow this by inhaling again as you turn hips left 90 degrees, moving weight to back left leg and undulating arms in a wave-like movement, then following this by moving weight back to right leg, pulling left leg into a Semi-T Stance and Grabbing the Ball.

(6) After which, do a (Slanted) Left-Hand Overhead Block with a Right-Hand Palm Thrust.

19. Needle at the Bottom of the Ocean (1 Breath)

(1) From Left-Leg Pointing Bow Stance of (Slanted) Left-Hand Overhead Block with a Right-Hand Palm Thrust (18/6)—

(2) Inhaling, pull back right foot up behind front left foot as left hand moves across front of body, sternum high, in a slow Left-Hand Cross Block to the right, right hand, palm open, dropping down then sliding up along the right side of the body.

(3–4) Then, beginning to exhale, move left leg out into a Right-Leg Supported Empty Stance as left hand, having finished Cross Block, now circles back, down, and to the left of the body where it stops, just below the hip, palm parallel to the plane of the floor, while right hand, having reached right shoulder, moves down directly in front of the body, fingers reaching down into an imaginary ocean.

Steps 2–4, a mirror image of 16 Postures, #12, Needle at the Bottom of the Ocean, Steps 2–4, complete a **Right-Hand Needle at the Bottom of the Ocean**, all in one breath.

20. Fan Through Back (1 Breath)

(1) From Right-Leg-Supported Empty Stance of Right-Hand Needle at the Bottom of the Ocean (19/4)—

(2) Inhaling, stand up, at the same time bringing left and right open hands toward body, sternum high, left palm up against inside of right wrist.

(3) Then, beginning to exhale, step out into a Left-Leg-Pointing Bow Stance, left hand extending straight out about sternum height in a Palm Thrust, right hand moving off to the right, right elbow bent at about a 125-degree angle, right arm almost parallel with the plane of floor, palm open outward at about ear height.

The movements in Steps **2–3** complete what can be called a **Left-Hand Fan Through Back**, a mirror image of 16 Postures, #13, Fan Through Back, Steps **2–3**.

21. Moving Hammer Fist Block to Parry and Vertical Hammer Fist (2 Breaths)

(1) From Left-Leg-Pointing Bow Stance of Left-Hand Fan Through Back (20/3)—

(2) Inhaling, rock back, and begin a Right Twist by turning 90 degrees right and moving weight to the back right leg.

(3–4) Next, still inhaling, as you move weight back to left leg, turn another 90 degrees right, pull right leg in close, simultaneously bringing left hand up and over head, then down, while dropping right fist down under left hand, which is now parallel to the plane of the floor.

(5–6) Without pause, begin exhaling as you raise and then drop right leg down into a Right-Heel Empty Stance, simultaneously bringing right fist up inside left arm, around, and then down in a Right-Fist Moving Hammer Block, left hand still dropping and now stopping at the side, palm down and parallel to the plane of the floor.

(7) Then move ahead with Right Hook and Left Parry.

(8) Followed by a Right Vertical Hammer Fist (in a Left-Leg-Pointing Bow Stance).

For help in remembering movements, transfer of weight, and breathing, reference the explanations for movements in 12 Basic Moves, #10, Moving Hammer Fist Block to Parry and Vertical Hammer Fist, Steps 8–12, and 16 Postures, #6, Moving Hammer Fist Block to Parry and Vertical Hammer Fist, Steps 3–6.

22. Bow Stance Push (1 Breath)

(1) From Left-Leg-Pointing Bow Stance of Right Vertical Hammer Fist (21/8)—

(2–3) Do two-handed Bow Stance Push.

Reference 12 *Qigong* Breathing Techniques, #9, Bow Stance Push, and 16 Postures, #7, Bow Stance Push, for details on coordinating movement, transfer of weight, and breathing.

23. Return (2 Breaths)

(1) From Left-Leg-Pointing Bow Stance of Bow Stance Push, arms/hands still extended (22/3)—

(2–6) Do Right-Leg Return, ending in Separation Stance.

Reference the exact same movements in 10 Postures, #10, Return and Closing, Steps 2–6, for details on coordinating movement, transfer of weight, and breathing.

24. Closing (1 Breath)

(1) From Separation Stance after Right-Leg Return (23/6)—

(2) Do Closing, paying attention to correct breathing.

5

Summary

The system of Taiji introduced in this book has been presented in a straightforward and step-by-step manner. Preceded by historical and philosophical background information, the goal of which is to very generally clarify the origins and nature of Taiji, this system starts with a simple warm-up, is followed by short introductions to stances, hand techniques, breathing, steps, and basic moves, and ends with the four easiest New Style Forms, those series of moves which, when practiced in accordance with the Principle of Opposites, aim at harmonizing movement and breathing, creating, in the process, the fluid and rhythmical form so characteristic of Taiji. A list of the Ten Essential Principles one should follow when practicing Taiji is also delineated. And online videos are provided for most learning stages, along with still shots and precise descriptions for many moves. All of this combines to provide learners with a minimum, good, one-hour daily workout.

Although it originated in martial arts and still retains techniques and skills readily adapted to fighting and self-defense, the reader might now well agree that the combination of concentration, breathing, and movement in what was called the "three-part dialectic of meditation" clearly demonstrates that Taiji shares a common matrix of action with classic Indian Yoga. It can, therefore, be seen as a moving form of meditation. Moreover, Taiji as introduced in this short book should be seen as a unique form of exercise, one not difficult to learn, and one that, when learned correctly, will help practitioners cultivate vigor, strength, and wellness of the body, serenity and a sense of calm in the mind. Two hundred and fifty million practitioners worldwide are not wrong. Whether you are a beginner, intermediate, or advanced practitioner, whether you are young or old, physically agile or limited in your movements, Taiji, the future of fitness, can be your simple way to a better life.

References

Chen Xin (1849–1929). (1997a) "Categorized Recordings of Chen Xin's Discussions on *Taijiquan*." Chinese version. In "Discussions on Chen-style *Taijiquan* 3," chapter 5 of "Chen-style *Taijiquan*," *The Complete Book of Taijiquan*, pp.260–285. Beijing: People's Physical Education Publishing.

Chen Xin. (1997b) "Recordings of Chen Xin on the Thirteen Organs and Body Parts." Chinese version. In "Discussions on Chen-style *Taijiquan* 4," chapter 5 of "Chen-style *Taijiquan*," *The Complete Book of Taijiquan*, pp.285–292. Beijing: People's Physical Education Publishing.

Chen, Yanling. (1995a) "The Importance of Yi and Chi in Tai Chi Chuan." English version. Trans. by Tchong Ta-Tchen. From Laurens Lee (ed.) and Kam Ray and Tchong Ta-Tchen, *The Annotated Theoretical and Practical Tai Chi Chuan*. Beijing: Chinese Tai Chi Chuan Association. Last accessed on 11/12/2018 at www.itcca.it/peterlim/imptyi.htm.

Chen, Yanling. (1995b) "Tai Chi Chuan Method of Breathing and Chi Direction." English version. Trans. by Tchong Ta-Tchen. From Laurens Lee (ed.) and Kam Ray and Tchong Ta-Tchen, *The Annotated Theoretical and Practical Tai Chi Chuan*. Beijing: Chinese Tai Chi Chuan Association. Last accessed on 11/12/2018 at www.itcca.it/peterlim/tcbreath.htm.

Editorial Committee, People's Physical Education Publishing (PPEP). (1997a) "Harmonizing Inhalations and Exhalations." Chinese version. In "Rules that Must be Observed When Making Frames, Section 3," chapter 5 of "Simple Introduction to Wu-style *Taijiquan*," *The Complete Book of Taijiquan*, pp.474–475. Beijing: People's Physical Education Publishing.

Editorial Committee, People's Physical Education Publishing (PPEP). (1997b) "The Operation of *Yi* and *Qi* under the Control of the Thorax." Chinese version. In "The Eight Special Characteristics of *Taijiquan*, First Special Characteristic," chapter 1 of "Chen-style *Taijiquan*," *The Complete Book of Taijiquan*, pp.6–11. Beijing: People's Physical Education Publishing.

Eliade, Mircea. (1969) *Yoga: Immortality and Freedom*. Bollingen Series LVI. Princeton: Princeton University Press.

Yang, Chengfu (1883–1936). (1997a) "Talk about Practicing *Taijiquan*." Recorded by Zhang Hongkui. Chinese version. From chapter 1 of "Yang-style *Taijiquan*," *The Complete Book of Taijiquan*, pp.311–313. Beijing: People's Physical Education Publishing.

Yang, Chengfu. (1997b) "Discussions on the Ten Essentials of *Taijiquan*." Recorded by Chen Weiming. Chinese version. From chapter 1 of "Yang-style *Taijiquan*," *The Complete Book of Taijiquan*, pp.314–315. Beijing: People's Physical Education Publishing.